CELLPHONE

CELLPHONE
The Story of the World's Most Mobile Medium and How It Has Transformed Everything!

PAUL LEVINSON

palgrave
macmillan

First published 2004 by
PALGRAVE MACMILLAN™
175 Fifth Avenue, New York, N.Y. 10010 and
Houndmills, Basingstoke, Hampshire, England RG21 6XS
Companies and representatives throughout the world

PALGRAVE MACMILLAN is the global academic imprint of the Palgrave Macmillan division of St. Martin's Press, LLC and of Palgrave Macmillan Ltd. Macmillan® is a registered trademark in the United States, United Kingdom and other countries. Palgrave is a registered trademark in the European Union and other countries.

ISBN 1–4039–6041–0 hardback

Library of Congress Cataloging-in-Publication Data

Levinson, Paul
    Cellphone / Paul Levinson
        p. cm.
    Includes bibliographical references and index
    ISBN 1–4039–6041–0
    1. Cellular telephone systems—Popular works. 2. Cellular telephones—Popular works. I. Title.

TK6570.M6L44 2004
303.48'33—dc22   2003066366

A catalogue record for this book is available from the British Library.

Design by Newgen Imaging Systems (P) Ltd., Chennai, India.

10 9 8 7 6 5 4 3 2

Printed in the United States of America.

Transferred to digital printing 2005

To Neil Postman
1931–2003
who taught me how to teach

Contents

List of Photographs
(of Postcards)

Preface
The Irresistible Calling

This is a medium-sized book about a little device with an enormous impact. We should not be surprised to find small packages doing big things in communications—our brain, after all, weighs about a kilogram. Cellphones lack the intelligence of brains, but they increasingly do or help us do any kind of communication our brain desires, anywhere our brains, and our bodies, happen to be.

The device is well named. In England and many parts of the world, it is called a mobile phone, but "cellphone" is better. Because it not only travels, like organic cells do, but, also like cells, it can generate new communities, new possibilities and relationships, wherever it happens to be. The cellphone, in other words, is not only mobile, but generative, creative. And the word "cell" works in another way as a description of what the cellphone does. For it not only opens up possibilities, but pressures us to always be in touch. This aspect of the cellphone thus can imprison us in a cell of omni-accessibility.

Cellphone explores the nature and extent of this revolution and its impact on our lives, on love and war, on business and pleasure, and just about everything in between. The book begins with a discussion of some of these developments, and in Chapter 2 looks at some of the previous media that we carried with us—books, the Kodak camera, the transistor radio. Each of these got us out of the home, the studio, the office, and into the outside world. But the cellphone is unique, in that it gives us not only information, but conversation, anyplace we please.

The Internet usually is seen as the defining medium of our age. It is indeed the medium of media, giving us books, photographs, radio shows, e-mail, newspapers, magazines, and a myriad of other types of communication on our screen. But it exacts a price: the ticket for admission to cyberspace usually is being stuck in a seat behind a desk indoors. Chapter 3 explores how the cellphone unglues and frees us from our homes and offices and gets us back into the big, real world outside.

Even before the Internet began combining so many different media, the home served as a hearth or central station for communication, offering not only conversation with family but telephone, radio, television, books, magazines, and newspapers. By giving us the Internet and all its media on the move, including telephone conversation, the cellphone makes each person who carries one a mobile hearth. The result is a telepathic, instantly omni-communicating society, which we consider in Chapter 4.

Not every impact of the cellphone is beneficial, and we examine some of its social drawbacks in Chapters 5 through 7. The capacity to call anyone anytime we like, and to be called by people we want to hear from, also allows us to be called anytime, anywhere, by people we may not want to talk to, at least not at that time. How to be inaccessible without offending may be the major challenge of the cellphone age.

Talking on the cellphone in certain public places can also be irritating to eavesdroppers. Do they have a right to be annoyed? Chapter 6 examines the reasons for this rash of annoyance, in what places it most frequently appears, and what, if anything, could and should be done about it.

Parents and children, husbands and wives, are among the most affected by the cellphone. Chapter 7 hefts and ponders the two-edged sword of the cellphone for family life. Kids love the cellphone because it enables them to call their friends outside of the home and away from parental ears; but it also allows parents to call them anytime, anywhere. Infidelity may become more difficult due to the cellphone, but it makes nagging easier. The home had already been colonized by business due to the telephone and the Internet. The cellphone is now homogenizing the office with home.

Chapter 8 returns to the nonvocal uses of the cellphone. In some parts of the world, text messages are more common on cellphones than spoken conversations. This makes sense—text can be more precise than speech, and also has the golden virtue of silence. And the use of the cellphone to access the Internet for information does not interfere with our need to be inaccessible: unlike a person you may talk to on the cellphone, the Internet is not likely to call you back at an inopportune time. In the long run, the Internet may well be seen as just a service of the cellphone. I would not be surprised if, a few years after I wrote this, you were reading this very book on your cellphone right now.

Chapter 9 looks at how the cellphone is erasing the digital divide, worldwide. It requires only inexpensive relay towers or satellites already in the sky, which means that poorer nations all over the world can be part of the cellphone community. And this in turn means that a cellphone in a traveler's pocket is likely to work in more and more places around the world. The Internet already made Marshall McLuhan's global village interactive. The cellphone gets the villagers out of their seats, onto their feet, and moving through the world.

The 2003 Iraqi War took place as I was completing this book. The role of the cellphone in both the reporting and the very conduct of that war is examined in Chapter 10. The embedded reporter, outfitted with a cellphone and a video hookup to a television broadcast, continues and revolutionizes a tradition of battlefield media that began with the Civil War photography of Mathew Brady; the use of cellphones in "decapitation" strikes on enemy leaders refines another enlistment of media that began in the Civil War with the use of the telegraph to direct troop movements.

The book concludes with a discussion of how the cellphone can be improved. Even before the cellphone, the telephone was the most improved instrument in media history, stocked with answering machines, call waiting, caller ID, and other remedies. Of course, like all technologies, these were trade-offs, and caused new problems (caller ID robs the caller of surprise) even as they solved old ones (caller ID obstructs the obscene caller). Two improvements for the cellphone—one of benefit to the caller, the other to the called—are suggested.

* * *

Note that this book offers little discussion about laws in some states that prohibit handheld cellphone use by drivers and no discussion at all of the claim that cellphone use can cause brain tumors. The claims are unsupported by medical evidence. As for the laws, there is no doubt that talking on the phone can be distracting for the driver. But whether laws or custom and education are the best way to handle this, and whether such laws are enforceable, are really questions that pertain to society and laws in general, not just to the cellphone. In general, about the cellphone as well as most other things, I take the view that evolution of custom is a better way of regulating personal and social behavior than enactment of laws.

Thus, *Cellphone* considers the historical context, social impact, and future possibilities of an instrument that lets us walk in the sunshine and talk to someone in the rain a continent away. Although we can always shut the cellphone off, if we wish, the ring of the phone always has been irresistible, and so too will be the cellphone's transformation of our lives and culture.

* * *

A word about the format of *Cellphone*: In the interest of keeping this book short and pithy, if not necessarily always sweet, I have dispensed with the scholarly custom of footnotes. I also have tried to keep references in the text to a minimum. On occasion, you will see some parenthetical remarks, which I found too pertinent or interesting to omit. Consider these subtexts, or, in cellphone parlance, textings, that I'm sliding in under and between the overt conversation.

For those who relish the nooks and crannies of sources, I have also included a Select Bibliography at the end of the book, with extensive annotations. This can be read either as flash-forwards from parts in the book where the references are cited or as a self-sufficient, somewhat alternate way in itself of looking at the cellphone.

And speaking of looking at the phone, I have also included in Chapters 1 and 7 a series of photographs of early twentieth-century postcards that portray the public's perception of the phone at that time. The postcards are from my private collection.

* * *

I was very fortunate to have three talented editors at various stages of this project: Kristi Long, with whom I first broached the idea for a book about the cellphone; Roee Raz, who made some very helpful comments after reading an early, short draft; and Farideh Koohi-Kamali, as well as her assistant, Melissa Nosal, who saw the book through to completion.

And, as always, I have had the best "first readers" in the world—who were this time, moreover, past masters in the subject of this book. Thanks to my wife, Tina, and our children, Simon and Molly, for their sage and insightful advice. And thanks to Tina, as well, for her sharp-eyed help with this book's copyediting and proofreading.

—Paul Levinson
New York City
December 2003

Chapter 1
The "Miracle-Phone"

It's called the "Pele-Phone"—"miracle-phone"—in Israel, where more than 75 percent of the people have one. It's the name of one of Israel's biggest cellphone companies, and more than a clever play on words. Certainly the ability to speak to anyone, anywhere, anytime, wherever you and he or she may be seems miraculous. Or at least it did ten years ago. Today the cellphone has become so ubiquitous that its wonders to behold are commonplace, an astonishing part of everyday life.

Yet it can make a life-and-death difference. On September 11, 2001, only three of the four hijacked planes crashed into buildings. The fourth was annihilated in the Pennsylvania countryside, but it took the lives of only those in the plane. The terrorists on United Airlines flight 93 had not counted on the cellphone. Passengers on that plane, informed by their loved ones of the World Trade Center attacks, were able to take action.

The cellphone has been a life-saver, a seeming miracle from on high, more than once since then. On May 26, 2003—Memorial Day in the United States—a small plane went down in Long Island Sound. The pilot called for help on his cellphone; he couldn't describe his position; the Coast Guard told him to set off a flare, which he did, and he was found. Sometimes the cellphone comes only tragically close to making a difference. Four teenaged boys who drowned in their small boat off of City Island in New York in 2002 placed a call to 911 on a cellphone. In that case, unfortunately, the 911 operator failed to take effective action. Even the cellphone cannot always eliminate the toll of human error.

From its beginnings more than a century ago, Alexander Graham Bell's telephone was perceived by the public as a vehicle of miracles. Postcards from the early 1900s depict little girls talking to their deceased mothers in heaven—via the telephone.

One, entitled "Please, Miss, Give Me Heaven" (published by Bamford & Co., with "kind permission of Chas. K. Harris"), comes with this poetic caption:

> If you please, Miss, Give Me Heaven, for my Mamma's there,
> You will find her with the Angels on the golden stair;
> She'll be glad it's me who's speaking, call her, won't you
>   please?
> For I want to surely tell her we're so lonely here.

Another, entitled "If You Please, Miss, Give Me Heaven" (also published by Bamford, with the "kind permission" of Harris) continues the story:

> When the girl received this message
> Coming o'er the telephone,
> How her heart thrilled in that moment,
> And the wires seemed to moan;
> I will answer, just to please her,
> Yes, dear heart, I'll soon come home;
> Kiss me, Mamma, kiss your darling,
> Through the telephone.

The much-appreciated Mr. Harris—songwriter of the famous "After the Ball"—had written a well-known song, "Hello Central, Give Me Heaven." (See Figures 1.1 and 1.2.)

Bell Telephone was quick to see the great things the world expected of the phone, and around 1910 it issued a series of advertising postcards that touted the telephone, if not as a conveyor of miracles, at least as an essential lifeline. One card, entitled "A Doctor Quick by Bell Telephone," shows a nurse in the home of a stricken family, summoning a doctor by

Figure 1.1. "Please Miss, Give Me Heaven"

phone. Another, "The Bell Telephone Guards the Home by Night as by Day," depicts two women huddled in a darkened home by a phone, with a burglar lurking outside; an inset shows they are phoning the police. A third, "The Bell Telephone Gives Instant Alarms," portrays a woman trapped in her smoky bedroom, on the phone; a fire engine with bright

IF YOU PLEASE, MISS, GIVE ME HEAVEN.

When the girl received this message
Coming o'er the telephone,
How her heart thrilled in that moment,
And the wires seemed to moan;
I will answer, just to please her,
Yes, dear heart, I'll soon come home;
Kiss me, Mamma, kiss your darling,
Through the telephone.

By kind permission of Chas. K. Harris   Copyright

Figure 1.2. "If You Please, Miss, Give Me Heaven"

red wheels and three white horses is rushing over at breakneck speed. (See Figures 1.3, 1.4, and 1.5.)

The best the telegraph could do for emergencies, in an era prior to the advent of the telephone, was provide "call boxes" attached to walls in homes, with numbered, circular dials (predecessors of the rotary phone dial) that could send signals to

Figure 1.3. "A Doctor Quick By Bell Telephone"

Figure 1.4. "The Bell Telephone Guards the Home by Night as by Day"

Figure 1.5. "The Bell Telephone Gives Instant Alarms"

the local telegraph office (the American District Telegraph [ADT] Office). Twisting dial number one would prompt the ADT to request that a fire engine be sent to the home; dial number two would result in a prompt visit from the police; number three would yield a courier, who would hand-deliver a written message to the telegraph offices, to be sent out in Morse code over the wires. These sorts of arrangements were, of course, a lot better than nothing, and practically miraculous in their own right, but they lacked the vocal subtlety, precision, and immediate interactivity of the phone call, in which a patient's symptoms could be described exactly, and the doctor at the other end could ask questions.

Other postcards in the Bell Telephone series emphasize not quite life-and-death, but the flexibility and range of the telephone as an indispensable convenience: "Use the Bell Telephone When Servants Fail You," "The Bell Telephone Keeps The Traveler in Touch with Home," "Into the Heart of the Shopping District by Bell Telephone," "The Convenience of Marketing by Bell Telephone" (a mother with a baby is calling her grocer), and the like.

But nonetheless, not everyone appreciated the telephone. Its capacity to access the world meant that the world could access you. The sanctity of the Victorian home was shattered, at least insofar as voices calling you. In England, the telephone took decades longer to catch on than in America, in part because of concerns about privacy. Even a majority of Americans would not have phones in their homes until the 1950s. One virtue of the public pay phone was that you could walk away from it. Dinners and lovemaking were not subject to its interjections. No telephone advertisements depicted a family at dinner or a couple in bed—interrupted by a ringing phone.

Today, the cellphone has carried this two-edged sword of access from our offices and homes to anywhere we may sit, walk, or travel. Its wireless miracles come with strings attached.

Trade-Offs

All communication media are trade-offs. The written word conveys the voice of an absent person, as Sigmund Freud noted. But the absent voice of writing did not respond immediately to questions, as Socrates observed more than two millennia earlier. Nowadays, the written word in e-mail (and instant messaging) can indeed be used for a kind of conversation. But it is less permanent than words on paper, and more vulnerable to prying eyes. Are these losses offset, more than exceeded, by the benefits of e-mail? Yes. Otherwise, e-mail would not have survived. The ability to correspond with someone anywhere in the world instantly is a net improvement in communication. But this does not mean that e-mail has no disadvantages. Keeping them in focus may help us reduce them, and thereby increase the net advantage of e-mail.

The cellphone is not only a net improvement in communication, it is an improvement over communication on the

Net—in communication on the Internet, and its general requirement, until recently, that its users be seated at desks, in front of screens. For all of its revolutionary impact, the Internet was utterly conventional in what media theorists call "conditions of attendance"—the physical surroundings in which consumers reap its benefits. Like traditional television and telephone, the Internet insisted that its users be immobile. Indeed, the Internet was even more demanding about this than prior media—landline telephone allows pacing around a room, and TV permits quick trips to the refrigerator during commercials. Unless you are in the middle of a long download or upload, the Internet ceases its service to you the instant you leave its presence.

In contrast, the cellphone cuts the room-leash completely. Like the Kodak camera, ballpoint pen, and transistor radio before it, the cellphone brings its users out of the home, out of the office, into the promised land of the world at large. The Palm Pilot is thus as much a child of the cellphone as of the personal computer. Indeed, the perspective of this book is that, in the long run, the Internet may be seen as an adjunct of the cellphone. Physical mobility-plus-connectivity through the world—what the cellphone brings us—may be more revolutionary than all the information the Internet brings to us in rooms.

But if mobility is the name of the cellphone's benefits, it is also the source of its liabilities. Laws against using a handheld cellphone while driving an automobile point to the worst of these problems. If you are already in high-speed motion, in a situation that requires your attention and your hands on the wheel, then the advantage of the cellphone becomes just the reverse. It can kill you and others; its lifeline can become a noose. The social disruptions caused by the cellphone in other situations—calls unwanted by you, conversations unappreciated by bystanders—pale in comparison.

But the fact that laws have been enacted to prohibit use of handheld cellphones by drivers brings home a very important lesson about media trade-offs. We need not sit mute, powerless, passive in response to the drawbacks and dangers of otherwise beneficial media. We can deploy newer technology—remedial media, such as headsets for cellphones—to reduce some of the ill effects. We can create social expectations, culminating in laws, if necessary, to regulate behavior. Neither is a perfect solution. The driver who uses a handless cellphone still may be distracted from the highway at a crucial moment by a demanding or scintillating conversation. And laws, of course, can be disobeyed. But both are part of a saving cytoplasm in which the future of the cellphone and its nucleus of mobility will circulate.

Unintended Consequences and Remedial Media

The cellphone itself is a remedial medium for one of the unintended consequences of the Internet—which replaced a lot of stationery, but kept us stationary. But the cellphone has unintended consequences all its own. Calls can arrive at unwanted times; cellphones with cameras can take photos of friends and strangers in compromising positions.

This tug of war, or seesaw, between unintended consequences and remedial technology (and law) runs throughout human history and media. Look at the window: It was invented in the first place as a remedy for holes in walls, which were themselves hit upon as an improvement over just walls, and their lack of views. But holes in the wall cost us cold and rain in the face for the view of the outside they afforded. Hence the remedial medium of the window, which gave us the outside, or a look at it, without the elements. But the wonderful window created new problems—annoyances of unwanted access—foreshadowing some of the current problems with the cellphone. The same window that allowed us to comfortably look out, allowed people outside our home to comfortably look in. In other words, the window spawned the Peeping Tom. But we came up with yet a new remedy for this new problem—curtains, window shades,

Venetian blinds, which not only give us privacy when pulled down and closed, but also allow us to peek through the window without being seen. We have not yet come up with quite such a Venetian blind for callers we do not want to hear from on our cellphones. (Shutting the phone off is like walking away from the window; caller ID and different rings keyed to different callers are a start, but even hearing the ring of an incoming call we *do* wish to receive can be distracting.) But the venerable process of remedial media suggests that we will come up with a better blind for the cellphone.

Thomas Edison, a veritable one-man age of invention, is a textbook example of unintended consequences and remedies. His first thought about the phonograph, which he stumbled onto in 1877, a year after Alexander Graham Bell's invention of the telephone, was that the sound recorder would make a marvelous adjunct to the telephone—a "telephone repeater," as he termed it, which could provide recordings of all that traversed the phone. He, of course, was thinking about the remedial medium of the telephone answering machine, but was about a hundred years premature. Instead, the phonograph went its own, unintended way and began thriving as a camera of music. Emile Berliner was quick to see (and hear) this, and Edison soon realized, too, that recordings of musical performances were a natural and profitable application of his invention. Indeed, so much so that, when Edison developed one of the first motion picture processes a decade later, his first thought was that it could offer a photographic accompaniment for music recordings, so the listener would have a motion picture of the singer or performer. And, once again, Edison was right, but, again, a hundred years too early. His initial vision for motion pictures would become today's music video. And, in Edison's time and throughout the twentieth century and into the present, the motion picture instead became a vehicle of novel-length narratives, in which recorded music served as an accompaniment rather than vice versa.

Edison's error in initially not seeing the huge success of the music recording and motion picture industries he engendered is not a case of idiosyncratic myopia. Rather, it is an indication of the intrinsically unpredictable applications and consequences of all media—unpredictable, at least, to many of their inventors. This pattern was recognized at least as far back as Socrates, who recounts, in the *Phaedrus* (section 275), the observation of a then-ancient Egyptian king, Thamus, that "he who has the gift of invention is not always the best judge of its utility or inutility of his own inventions to the users of them."

And yet the sound recording as a remedy for the fleeting telephone call and conversation, the motion picture as a remedy for the faceless singer on the phonograph recording, did come to be, eventually. Who made that happen? The same aggregate of human choice that sent the phonograph and the motion picture off on their destinies, different from their inventor's expectations, in the first place.

Democratic, Darwinian Media

People determine the evolution of media—which ones survive, which ones fall by the wayside, which ones hang on by a thread, which ones thrive. By "people," I mean neither captains of industry nor totalitarian dictators. Were the future of media determined by such powerful people, William Orton's mighty Western Union Telegraph Company would not have been gobbled up by Bell's start-up telephone company, after Orton had declined to buy all rights in the telephone for $100,000 in 1877, and then counseled his friend Chauncey Depew to pass up an opportunity to acquire one-sixth of all Bell Telephone rights into perpetuity for $10,000 in 1881. Orton was sure that the phone was a "toy," with no "commercial possibilities." Nor, if dictatorial political leaders rather than CEOs had any more ultimate influence on the survival of media, would underground "samizdat" video and photocopying have spread like wildfire in the Soviet Union. (See S. H. Hogarth's "Three Great Mistakes," 1926, for more on the hapless Mr. Depew, who also turned down an offer to seek the Republican

Party nomination for president in 1888, on the grounds that the Democratic incumbent, Grover Cleveland, was unbeatable. Republican Benjamin Harrison went on to oust Cleveland in that election, even though Harrison, like George W. Bush in 2000, lost the popular vote. John Brooks' *Telephone: The First Hundred Years*, 1976, provides a good overview of the economic wranglings surrounding the early telephone, and the evolution of the public's perception of the phone in what may now be called its pre-cellphonic century. See also my "Samizdat Video Revisited," 1992, for more on the inability of totalitarian leaders to dictate the evolution of media.)

In Darwinian terms, media compete for our attention—our time, our patronage, our purchase. Every time we decide to go out to the movies rather than stay at home and watch television, read a book rather than watch a video, talk on the cellphone rather than send e-mail, we are making a tiny contribution to the rise and fall of media. We are acting as the selecting environment for species of media. We might say that media evolve not by natural selection, but by our selection—or the natural choices of humans. The survival of the fittest media means the survival of media that most fit our needs. Intentions of inventors and decisions of political and business leaders have proven not very relevant to this process in the long run.

Millionaires, of course, can make a bigger splash than paupers. The rich and powerful not only can select media more frequently—can make a hundred purchases or media choices, to the average Joe and Jane's handful—but the wealthy also can create companies to market media, which bring them to the attention of more people, who can then select the media presentations and services. But anyone who has access to any kind of medium—whether pencils and paper clips or skywriting planes—anyone who can opt to respond or not to its messages has a hand on some part of the oar. And over the long haul, more hands on the oar determine the direction of media evolution.

This does not necessarily mean that we are rowing in the right direction—that our media choices are good for us in our actual short-term or long-term interests. The law of unintended consequences weighs heavily here. When cellphones first hit the mass market in the 1990s, teenagers loved them—what a great way to stay in touch with friends! They soon discovered that their parents loved cellphones, too, because the little phones made it difficult for the kids to be out of touch. When it comes to unintended consequences, we are all of us children, for all media.

But the success of any medium, certainly the enormous success of the cellphone, means it has survived a human test. It satisfies some human need, whether superficial itch or profound longing. In the Darwinian stream, the fish that swims the fastest, has the best camouflage, snares the best prey, survives. The pebbles on the bottom may be a different color around the next bend and may turn the fish's camouflage into a bull's-eye—and the successful, nearly invisible fish into a clearly tempting target. There are no sure things, no guarantees, in evolution, be it natural or technological.

For the cellphone, however, the human need satisfied is not likely to change around the next bend, or anytime soon. It is a need as old as the human species—the need to talk and walk, to communicate and move, at the same time. It is a need that even defines the human species, as an organism that makes symbolically meaningful sounds with voice boxes and tongues, and goes from place to place upright, on hind legs.

In the next chapter, we begin our survey of the cellphone, its impact and its future, with a look at mobility and its history in human communication.

Chapter 2
Information on the Move

We can look just about anywhere in history and find precedent for people walking down the street and talking on the phone. Indeed, walking down the street, or path, or anywhere and just talking to the person right next to you is the ultimate, original precedent. We are, like all animals, a species on the move. Also, like all animals, and for that matter all forms of life, we communicate. But unlike any other life that we know about, we speak, and yearn to speak to people not in our physical presence.

Speech—abstract, symbolic language—is key in this. Unlike a drawing on a cave wall or a pictograph, the spoken word looks like nothing. And therefore it can stand for, represent, describe, anything we please. Therein lies its great power. Our ancestors who were able to say to their friends and family, "Hey, there's a very hungry, vicious, bloodthirsty lion a few miles from here, and it's headed in our direction!" had a big advantage over their hominid relatives who could only grunt and gesture and shriek to their friends and family about the danger. We are the descendants of the bands that spoke. Those hominid species that did not speak probably contributed more to the lions' survival than to their own in the long run.

And if we can talk about anything on our mind, whether it is right in front of us or not, we can talk not only about lions but other people who are far away. And from there it is a minor step for us not only to talk about people we are thinking about, but to think about talking to people we are thinking about, however far away they may be.

When you add to this the natural desire to talk to people far away, not only wherever they are, but wherever we are, you arrive, almost inevitably, at the cellphone: the ability to talk and walk at the same time, regardless of where we are walking and regardless of where the person we are talking to is walking.

Walking is also crucial here. According to anthropologists, walking played as large a part as talking in our emergence as human beings. Perhaps even before we talked, our ancestors stood up and walked. We are the only bipedal mammal. Using just two of our four limbs to walk freed our other pair of limbs—our hands—to do and hold things. Like the cellphone.

When we walked out of Africa and talked about it, we were thus headed slowly but surely for the cellphone. Intelligence and inventiveness, applied to our need to communicate regardless of where we may be, led logically and eventually to telephones that we carry in our pockets.

There were other devices of communication that we carried in our pockets, or hands, or on arms and shoulders, prior to the cellphone. None was interactive, however. None allowed us to have a conversation with someone not right next to us—one of the two crucial characteristics of the cellphone. But they were nonetheless portable—the other crucial capacity of the cellphone—and on that account can be considered non-interactive, portable precedents of the cellphone.

The first time someone thought to write on a tablet that could be lifted and hauled—rather than on a cave wall, a cliff face, a monument that usually was stuck in place, more or less forever—we were in the media-in-motion business. Moses was wise to bring the Ten Commandments down from the mountain on tablets. They could be carried not only through the desert, but eventually to the entire world.

Streamlining of all aspects of the writing process sped the flow of information. The Ten Commandments were written in a phonetic alphabet rather than pictographic hieroglyphics—the alphabet was easier to learn (a few handfuls of symbols in comparison to hundreds of pictographs), and its letters could represent an all-powerful, all-present, invisible monotheistic deity as easily as they could indicate a four-legged animal that barked. In centuries that followed, papyrus, parchment, and paper lightened the burden of tablets. Pens, paintbrushes, and pencils were easier to wield than chisels. Roman roads became major arteries for written documents. (See my book *The Soft Edge: A Natural History and Future of the Information Revolution*, 1997, for more on the history of writing and its social consequences.)

The Dark Ages in Europe occluded those vessels of information with centuries of neglect and misapprehension. But the Renaissance brought forth an invention that till this day remains one of the marvels of media mobility: the printed book. Although prior to the printing press handwritten documents were easy enough to transport, they required considerable time, attention, and talent to reproduce. The result was that dissemination of information even in the best of the handwritten ages—Hellenistic and Roman civilizations—was severely limited by tight spigots. The burnings of the Library of Alexandria by the Christian bishop Theophilus in A.D. 390 and again by Muslim forces in A.D. 640 thus destroyed something more valuable than just 400,000 books (a conservative estimate for Alexandrian holdings; higher estimates place the number of books lost at 700,000): lost in the flames were books of which there was but one copy. In contrast, the printing press, invented in China around A.D. 700 and deployed with movable type by Gutenberg in Europe about 700 years later, reproduced thousands upon thousands of copies of individual books. The information they conveyed was soon in almost as many places as the DNA in our cells.

Thus the words on the pages of books were now resistant to eradication. Once distributed, multiple copies were beyond total recall, whether by Hitler's book burnings in the twentieth century or any other means. The printing press let the cat of information out of the bag forever—or, for at least as long as there remain humans, somewhere, with the capacity to read the printed, book-bound words.

And the book, any printed page, was and continues to be amenable to delivery of its information—to being read—in the widest variety of places and circumstances. From the vantage point of the twentieth and twenty-first centuries, and their requirement of electrical power and special equipment for the enjoyment of radio, television, and computers, the products of the printing press are incredibly generous in their request for nothing more than the light already provided by the world. During the day, books, newspapers, and magazines come with batteries included. Even in the evening, if moonlight doesn't do, the light from ubiquitous non-communication technologies works just fine. (Historian David de Haan aptly observed that "electricity did more to facilitate the habit of reading books than anything before it.") Ambient light—or light everywhere—makes the ambient book readable anywhere. All that is needed is a literate human being.

Literacy thus became the prime prerequisite of all mobile—and stationary—written communication. It was far more difficult to come by than daylight, and far more expensive to attain, in both time and money, than any specific product of the press, such as a book. Even a costly, difficult-to-locate tome usually can be obtained for hundreds of dollars after months of searching. But if the tome cost a thousand dollars and took years to locate, this would still be less than the expense of learning how to read, which can take a good decade (at least, to get to the level of being able to read a tome with full comprehension) and thousands of dollars, if we consider the cost of formal schooling, whether paid for privately or through taxes.

But we spend this time and money precisely because literacy is so essential in a world of print (and, indeed, continues to be, in a world of Internet e-mail, instant messaging, and cellphone texting). There is a scene in the 1997 movie *The Matrix* that beautifully captures the significance of this prerequisite. Neo (a.k.a. Thomas A. Anderson, the hero) has been taken into custody and is being interrogated, harshly, by Agent Smith. Neo demands his right to a phone call. Smith (played by Hugo

Weaving) archly replies: "And tell me, Mr. Anderson, what good is a phone call if you are unable to speak?" And because (as we later learn) this whole conversation takes place in a virtual world, under Smith's control, Neo's mouth disappears.

In the decades and centuries after the deployment of the printing press in the West, people similarly asked themselves: And tell me, what good is a book or a newspaper if you can't read? The result was the rise of public education, which even today still has as its fundamental mandate the teaching of children how to read. But progress was slow. Not until the last decades of the nineteenth century would percentages of the literate in comparison to the overall population be as high in America as they were in the heyday of ancient Alexandria.

By then the technologies of both printing and writing also had been improved. The inculcation of literacy, after all, benefited the creation as well as the reception of writing. As more people learned how to read, the demand for books, newspapers, and, eventually magazines, increased. The number of readers and the number of things they could read were mutually catalytic—the growth of one stimulated the growth of the other, which in turn stimulated the growth of the first, which in turn stimulated the growth of the other. *The Times* of London started using a steam-driven press in 1814. By the 1830s, R. Hoe & Company in America had perfected this press to the point that it could produce four thousand double pages per hour. The cost of printing plummeted. The result was the penny press (newspapers that sold for a penny, in contrast to the previous six cents per copy), the advent of periodicals like *Harper's* (presses worked so quickly that they were often idle at the end of the week; publishers decided to use the time to print magazines), and the general informing of the Jacksonian "common man." Meanwhile, the shift-key typewriter, invented in 1878, with its upper- and lowercase letters, soon allowed individual writers to produce text almost as clear as the printer's.

But high-speed presses were still stationary, as were most early typewriters. For the person who wanted to write as well as read on the go—to pen a letter on a park bench, in a train terminal, anyplace away from home or office—the laptop desk or lap desk was the ideal contrivance: not only pens but inks, blotters, paper, and a firm writing surface were all folded up and ready to travel in this Victorian attaché case.

The world at the end of the nineteenth century was in a budding state of media mobility. The Kodak camera was already making its own contribution, and would be joined in the twentieth century by the transistor radio, the laptop computer, and the cellphone.

The Kodak Camera and the Mobile Media Producer

For all the book's potent portability, it pertains only to its consumers, not its producers. Nowadays, a writer can write just about as easily, anywhere, as a reader can read. But getting published on paper and distributed is quite another thing. The expense of printing and shipping mass amounts of paper, even with the continued improvement of technology and consequent reduction of costs, still is more than enough to limit the number of publishers in comparison to the number of readers. Photographic and then computer typesetting reduced some of the production bills, but made paper, binding, and shipping no less costly.

Publishing on the Web and "print-on-demand" single copies equalized the asynchronicity of production and consumption at the end of the twentieth century, but still accounted for only a small fraction of book and newspaper sales a decade later. Further, the book or newspaper on the Web lacks what I call "reliable locatability." The book of paper pages has a good chance of being in the same place we left it on the shelf a few hours, a few days, even a few years later (if the shelf is in our home); certainly what is on page 20 of the printed book you are currently holding in your hand still will be on page 20 whenever you look at the book, if it hasn't decomposed or been damaged. But the intrinsic nature of our computer screen is utterly different. It constantly changes—indeed, it is "refreshable," so changing is just what it is supposed to do. And the combination of broken and deliberately shifted links on the Web, at least at the beginning of the twenty-first century, makes it far less stable than anything printed on paper. Since ease of revision is one of the Web's great advantages, this unstable state is likely to continue. The price for easy revisability is loss of reliable locatability.

Photographs were as portable as books from the beginning, and nearly as enduring. They were intended to rescue an image, as the French film theorist André Bazin would later so aptly put it, from "its proper corruption in time" (see his *What Is Cinema?* 1967). The smallest daguerreotypes and ambrotypes in the 1840s and 1850s were even easier to carry than books. They fit in your pocket and weighed about the same as a cellphone. An antebellum Victorian would have been quite comfortable with a twenty-first century Nokia.

So the mid-nineteenth century knew the value of laps and pockets as vectors for at least a few media, including the photograph. The first cameras, however, were another matter—they were big, bulky, and transportable rather than portable (a good distinction, which I first heard in the early 1980s about early pre-laptop personal computers such as the Kaypro, which when packed up and ready to go weighed about twenty-five pounds; see Peter A. McWilliams, *The Personal Computer Book*, 1982, for detailed descriptions of Kaypros and other early personal computers). Early cameras also took considerable talent to operate. The result, as the first fifty years of the photograph's tenure unfolded, was a limited number of professionals taking photographs of almost everyone, to place on their mantels or carry in their vests. Although the imbalance between printer and reader was greater—cameras were far less expensive than presses—the photograph perpetuated the printed pattern of few producers and many consumers.

The Kodak camera in 1888 was the first modern medium to sharply reverse that trend, and indeed it was the first medium to empower mobile producers since the pen and its amanuensis, the laptop desk. With a little black box of a camera in hand—about the size of a laptop today—anyone could snap a picture. Just as the cellphone would move telephonic conversation out of the home and office into the world at large, so the Kodak a century earlier took the camera out of the professional studio and into everyone's vacations, birthday parties, and walks along the beach.

George Eastman coined the name "Kodak" because he wanted his invention associated with nothing else before it. And his instincts were apt. The name with no precedent was more than a clever marketing ploy. For the first time in history, images of the world could be captured by anyone, anytime, anywhere. Outfitted with the extension of the Kodak camera, the human eye could now not only see but record what it saw—not just in inexact, faulty memory, not just in the symbolic description (and inevitable distortion) of writing, but literally, exactly, totally, and anyplace the eye happened to gaze. Of course, the camera could miss part of the scene, just as the eye could. But it recorded, faithfully and completely, whatever passed into its lens.

And unlike the pen and the lap desk and the writing they made possible, which was still difficult on cold and windy days outdoors, a quick snapshot with the Kodak was a breeze in most kinds of weather. The new mobile cameras were truly denizens of the wide world.

But writing and photography did have a common denominator: both catered to vision. The next revolution in mobility would play to the ear.

Radio on Wheels

Of the two great acoustic inventions of the nineteenth century—the electronic telephone in 1876 and the mechanical phonograph in 1877—at first only the phonograph contributed to the mobility of media. Indeed, early crank-driven "talking machines" were not only players but recorders, and thus were full-fledged Kodaks of sound. But the recordings themselves progressed through a series of cumbersome cylinders and heavy but fragile disks, which were more difficult to carry than books and photographs. Easy mobility in recordings would await the 45-rpm vinyl of the 1950s—released just a few years after radios had begun to make a big impact in cars.

The records and the radios played rock 'n' roll. The music was well suited to the decade and its unfurling of the Interstate Highway System. It was a music devoted to motion. The very words "rock 'n' roll" whispered, shouted, spoke of motion. Named after African American slang for sexual intercourse— rockin' and rollin' the night away makes more sense, once the linguistic origins of the term are understood—the music also had a driving four-four beat that was perfect for fast dancing. (I never could figure, as a kid, just what Bill Haley and the Comets were so excited about, rockin' round the clock. Once I learned the origin of the term "rock," I understood.)

Driving is an apt word here, too, because the radio in the automobile was of special benefit to the driver. Cars and radios had been invented around the same time—the turn of the twentieth century—but it would take until 1929 for Transitone to introduce the first car radio and twenty more years before the radio became standard automotive equipment. Books and cameras, for all their portability, were of no use to the driver, who could afford to look through neither pages nor lenses with the road looming ahead. Radio, in contrast, capitalized on our physiological capacity to hear one thing and see something else. It was and is ideal accompaniment and entertainment for anyone who needs to keep an eye on rapidly changing, potentially dangerous environments in motion.

The replacement of bulky vacuum tubes by sleek transistors not only sped the installment of radio in cars, but allowed strolling pedestrians to be entertained and informed by radio, too. Invented at AT&T's Bell Laboratories in 1948—and independently, a few months later, by two German physicists—the transistor triggered the start if not of the electronic information age (that distinction belongs to the telegraph, more than a century before), at very least the era of electronic media portability. This reduction in size and increase in power had been described as a general principle of technological development as early as the 1930s by Buckminster Fuller, who called it the "dymaxion" principle. (See Fuller's *Nine Chains to the Moon*, 1939. See Campbell's "Evolutionary Epistemology," 1974, and the sources cited there for the "ubiquity" of simultaneous, independent invention. That phenomenon, however, may be a casualty of McLuhan's global village, in particular its realization in the 1990s in cable television and the Internet, each of which spreads information worldwide at lightning speed. If there is nowhere in the world where a would-be inventor cannot hear about someone else's similar invention, then how can the new invention be independent?)

The human brain is a natural triumph and template of Fuller's dymaxion principle, processing vision, hearing, the other senses, thought, dreams, schemes, imaginings, plans, emotions, personality, intellect, mentality—maybe even the soul—all from the little kilogram of matter in our skulls, carried with ease on our legs. But the dymaxion would achieve its fullest technological expression—thus far—when the transistor was replaced by the microchip, which brought on the digital age. By the beginning of the twenty-first century, the most advanced computer chip would do the work of more than a billion transistors.

Laptops and Portable Production

We have followed two lines of media mobility in human history. One, including books and car radios, brought the products of communication to consumers on the move. The other, ranging from pencils to Kodak cameras, allowed people in all walks of life to be media producers. We tracked these two distinct lines of consumer and producer, of receiver and sender, of audience and creator, because they coincide and intertwine in the cellphone, which allows its users to both take and make calls—or be both consumers and producers of long-distance conversation.

As the twentieth century rounded its halfway mark, media that catered to consumption dominated all aspects of technologically assisted communication, stationary as well as mobile. For the average person—that is, someone not working as a producer in a media industry—the only media that could be used to create or initiate information were telephones, cameras (including recently invented photocopiers), and a variety of personal writing instruments ranging from crayons to typewriters. But telephones always came with earpieces as well as mouthpieces—that is, they receive as well as send. As a device of reception, the telephone performed like the venerable media of books and newspapers, and was joined in ensuing decades by such high-profile, one-way media of reception as motion pictures, radio, and television. Indeed, TV penetrated some 86 percent of American homes within a decade after its mass introduction in the late 1940s, a record in speed of public adoption equaled by no other medium, before or after. (The telephone took more than seventy-five years to penetrate more than 50 percent of American homes by the 1950s. The Web and the cellphone reached the 50 percent mark about a decade after their mass introductions, if one takes the date of their debuts as the early-to-mid-1990s. Neither medium has achieved 86 percent penetration as of this writing, in 2003.)

Prior to the advent of the Web as a mass, commercial medium, the personal computer—which, along with telephone lines, made the Web possible—caught on slowly but surely. By 1995 only about 30 percent of American households had computers. (This was about fifteen years after the personal computer made its entrance around 1980.) It is not surprising that the adoption of the personal computer was slow—far slower than that of television. Computers run on programs, and effective use of them, especially in the user-unfriendly early days, required considerable know-how. (In contrast to the different kind of "programs" on television, which require only open eyes and wakefulness to appreciate, and sometimes not even that. This, by the way, is not meant as a criticism of television, only a point of comparison with the personal computer. As I argued in my "Benefits of Watching Television," 1980, it is helpful and even healthy to have a medium at hand that requires so little of us. Human beings cannot be "on" all of the time.)

The personal computer required so much of us—a new kind of literacy, a "computer literacy," which assumed traditional reading-and-writing literacy and much more—because it bestowed powers of production. It was the first medium to do this since the telephone. The desktop computer was also a powerful instrument of reception, in its reading of information from disks and downloading of e-mail. But it facilitated writing and sending of information, as well. Not since the all-but-forgotten telegraph had electricity been brought into such massive service in the creation and dissemination of text. Sounds and images would follow shortly.

Unlike speaking on the telephone, however, all of this took considerable work. Learning how to use a computer was learning how to be a media producer—in a sense, like learning how to shoot a film, though much less was required of the computer user. For the adult in the 1980s, mastering a computer was probably closest to learning how to drive, which, prior to the personal computer, was the final summit, the attainment of which signaled entry into at least the technological aspect of adulthood. For the child, learning how to use a personal computer suddenly put him or her on an equal or sometimes even superior footing to adults. I recall being at a friend's home— he was also a professor—in 1984. He asked me something about his Commodore 64 computer. I had been using a

Kaypro at the time—both were CP/M computers (the "operating system" in use, prior to MS-DOS)—and I thought I knew a little about Commodores. But apparently not enough. I started talking, when a little boy, about seven years old—a friend of the professor's son—piped up and proceeded to answer my friend's question far more accurately and lucidly than I.

All of this technological and social revolution was made possible by the microchip. Soon this more-from-less invention engendered computers that were not only personal but portable. The luggable Kaypro appeared in 1983, followed a year later by Radio Shack's M100, a true laptop at four pounds. It alas ran on an operating system, an underlying program language, that was incompatible with the DOS, Mac, and CP/M systems of the time. But by the end of the decade, laptops with operating systems thoroughly compatible and interchangeable with desktops were widespread. Laptops and desktops were talking, at least to each other, in text and programs. In a few years, by the mid-1990s, they would be talking to the world in voices, as well.

But by that time so were cellphones, and far more effortlessly. Although the computer "interface"—another name for the operating or command system available to users—was far more friendly, and smiley, literally, than the austere exteriors of the 1980s, even the easiest, most "transparent" computer interface was far more demanding than what it took to make a cellphone call. By the mid-1990s the triumph of Windows meant that icons had replaced written command lines on DOS as well as on Mac computers (see my "Icons and Garbage Cans," 1992, for why this wasn't an unmixed blessing), but even the simplest point-and-click could take more doing than merely pressing a number and "Send" on your cellphone, especially when the target of your click was someplace on the Web.

Nonetheless, looked at one way, the last two decades of the twentieth century, and the twenty-first century thus far, can be seen as the age of personal computers. Indeed, personal computing and Web communication is what is usually meant by the "digital" age—word processing, data management, telecommunication in the beginning, moving on to cyberspace and the Web and all the business and play that it now encompasses. There is much truth in such a view. Shopping online, listening to MP3s and radio and watching movies on the Web, sending and receiving e-mail, instant messaging—these are indubitably digital, computer-based hallmarks of our age. In this perspective, the cellphone works as an important adjunct of our computer culture; the growing number of Internet functions available on cellphones can be seen as the cellphone's plugging in to and servicing the needs and expectations of an already computer-permeated world community.

But there is another way to look at this relationship. Although the personal computer's early word processing and data management capacities had nothing to do with the telephone, the telecommunicative power of the personal computer from the beginning has been entirely dependent on phone lines. Indeed, just as the telephone piggybacked on extensive telegraph lines already in place in the nineteenth century, so did the personal computer as a medium of communication take advantage of the telephone's infrastructure a century later. The modems that two decades of personal computers used to communicate modulated the digital information of computers into an analogic form capable of transmission through telephone lines, and then demodulated the analogic signals back into digital form, so as to be readable by the receiving computer (modem = MOdulation + DEModulation). As telephone lines themselves became digital in the twenty-first century, modems became unnecessary and gradually were replaced by faster devices that sent the digital data of computers directly through phone lines, without modulation and demodulation.

In this "telephonicentric" view, then, the computer can be seen as an adjunct of the telephone, rather than vice versa—at least insofar as the Web, cyberspace, e-mail, instant messaging,

Real Audio, MP3s, Amazon, all online shopping, and the like are concerned. The cellphone, then, becomes not only a better kind of telephone, but a better kind of Internet, which is unveiled as having been a special telephone with screens, written words, and images all along.

Dick Tracy, Captain Kirk, and the Gold Ingot

The personal computer received very little advance notice in popular culture—Murray Leinster's short story "A Logic Named Joe" (published in *Astounding Science Fiction* in March 1946) marks one of its few, early appearances. Instead, science fiction concentrated on artificial intelligence in robots and in huge mainframe computers. Robots of course move and in that sense are like laptops and palmtops, but they move— and think—of their own accord. They go back in our imagination at least as far as Rabbi Yehuda Loew's *Golem* in 1590 Prague, and wend their way through the organic form of the Frankenstein monster in the nineteenth century into a profusion of electronic beings, sometimes gleaming (robots), sometimes fleshlike (androids), brought forth by Isaac Asimov and many others in the twentieth century.

Because these robotic/humanoid creations can think for themselves, they are often beyond our control and become our undoing. As for the mainframe computer, it sometimes thinks for itself—to the benefit of humanity (as in Robert Heinlein's *Moon is a Harsh Mistress*, 1966) or otherwise (as in Asimov's "The Last Question," 1956)—but often does not. (On artificial intelligence thinking for itself, or being just a glorified pencil or appendage of our own intelligence, see J. R. Searle's "Mind, Brains, and Programs," 1980, and its distinction between "strong" and "weak" AI. I think this distinction is crucial but prefer the terms "autonomous" versus "auxiliary"; see my *Mind at Large: Knowing in the Technological Age*, 1988, for details.) The mainframe, or massive, stationary computing machine, appeared in fiction as early as 1879 (in Edward Page Mitchell's "The Ablest Man in the World") and in 1911 as a world wide web–like totalitarian system (E. M. Forster's "The Machine Stops"). Significantly, this was more than half a century after Charles Babbage starting sketching out serious plans for "difference" and "analytical" engines—computers—that were well publicized but never implemented, due to a lack of government support and necessary electronic technology. (Babbage worked in the tradition of Leonardo da Vinci, whose plans for helicopters—which likely would have flown—also were not realized in his time, for lack of appropriate metallurgy.) Like the robot, the mainframe weat on to blossom in popular culture in the 1940s and after. But, unlike the robot, this was probably because there were already real mainframe computers, behemoths with thousands of big vacuum tubes, running at that time. As with Mitchell's nineteenth-century story, science fiction about computers in the twentieth century was rooted in reality.

The fiction was not the only aspect of computers that was well rooted—for the mainframe may "run," internally, but it cannot move or be easily moved, if at all, and therefore it has even less in common than does the robot with laptops, PDAs, and cellphones. The mainframe and its culture is, rather, a precursor of the Internet, indeed the actual backbone of the Internet today, though the Web relies on numerous, far-flung mainframes (and other equipment), not just one.

The cellphone's sojourn in popular thinking, however, probably was closest to the mainframe's, at least insofar as major appearances in mass culture and partnership with actual developments in the laboratory and the street. Unlike Murray Leinster's "Joe," a kind of cellphone became known to millions in the 1940s via Dick Tracy and his two-way radio wristwatch. By the end of that decade, New York City had a wireless (radio) telephone network that could accommodate a total of twelve people talking at the same time. AT&T's Bell

Labs was pursuing a cellphone system that could serve hundreds of callers, but opted instead for car phone research. The difference was meaningful in those days: the bulk and weight and external antennas needed for the car phone could neither fit nor be carried in any pocket or pocketbook. The public saw a car phone in use in the 1954 movie *Sabrina*, when the millionaire played by Humphrey Bogart talked on the phone in the backseat of his limousine.

But the true cellphone, whether on wrist or in hand, was by no means forgotten. Indeed, it made what would become its best-known, most memorable appearance in popular fiction—certainly surpassing Dick Tracy by the twenty-first century—in the little beeping "communicators" used by Captain Kirk, Mr. Spock, and the crew of the *Starship Enterprise* on *Star Trek*. The NBC television series played from 1966 through 1969, but after it was canceled, it became wildly successful in the afterlife of reruns on syndicated TV stations around the country and the world, and engendered four additional television series and ten motion pictures as of 2003. As for the handy "communicator," what started as science fiction ended up, about three-quarters along the way from 1966 to 2003, widespread reality. In contrast, and as an indication of how devices in science fiction usually fare in our real world, the "transporter" or "beamer"—the teleportation device—also beloved by *Star Trek* fans ("Beam me up, Scotty!")—is as far away from real life today as it was in the 1960s.

With AT&T focusing on car phones, Motorola picked up the ball on a phone you could put in your pocket—a *Star Trek* "communicator" everyone could use. Martin Cooper, a science fiction devotee and director of research and development for Motorola, placed what is said to be the first public cellphone call on April 3, 1973—nearly four years after the original *Star Trek* series went off the air—from midtown Manhattan to a friendly rival scientist at Bell Labs in New Jersey. Motorola invested close to $100 million in the cellphone from the late 1960s to the early 1980s.

But the early models were hardly phones one could comfortably carry. They weighed almost two pounds, were shaped like gold ingots, and were worth nearly their weight in gold, too. Selling for about $4,000 in 1983, they were not comfortably affordable.

But, like the personal computer, which made its first major appearance a few years earlier (the Apple, in 1979) and was about to conquer the world with the IBM PC (1982), the price as well as the size of the cellphone would soon shrink. The economics are fundamental and apply to all new media. They cost a lot at first. A few wealthy people acquire them. At some point, the manufacturer realizes that if the price were lowered, a mass market could be created, with much more resulting net profit than at the higher price and fewer customers. In recent history this happened not only with personal computers and cellphones, but with VCRs and faxes. Longer ago, it happened with television, and longer ago than that, with books, a single copy of which cost an average working person's weekly salary in the year 1800—one dollar. (The same logic, alas and incidentally, still applies, in reverse, to scholarly books: If a publisher knows that a book has a very limited but almost guaranteed audience—as in the case of a book on any arcane topic, but still studied in the academy—the publisher will charge the proverbial arm and a leg for it. Presumably the book you are now reading cost less than that, since interest in the cellphone, its history, and its impact goes beyond—I hope—the arcane, scholarly audience.)

From 1985 to 2002, the number of cellular telephone subscribers in the United States grew from under 350,000 to nearly 150 million. This represents about two-thirds of American adults. (Interestingly, estimates in 2003 indicated that new cellphone subscribers are 60 percent more likely to be young adults than the general age of the overall population of non-subscribers.) In comparison, the number of Internet users in the United States was estimated at about 155 to 160 million. But whereas growth of the number of Internet users has been nil in the past few years—even dipping a bit in 2001—cellphone ownership and use has jumped nearly 30 percent in the same period of time. Figures around the world are even more favorable to the cellphone. (For a variety of sources, see the Cellular Telecommunications and Internet Association, Nielsen Net Ratings, Scarborough Research, and Clint Swett's 2003 article, "The Ubiquitous Cellphone Turns 30.")

The view that the cellphone is rapidly catching up to the Internet and soon will subsume it—meaning that laptops and Palm Pilots and all the news, music, images, and cornucopia of other information we receive from them will soon be accessible through our cellphones, in addition to the conversation, texting, photography, and television shows we now enjoy—seems warranted. Indeed, even pornography, long the most frequently viewed and downloaded pages on the Web (with the brief exception of MP3 music files, when they first became available on the Internet in the late 1990s), will soon make an appearance via downloadable *Playboy* pictures and video clips on new, "third-generation" European cellphones, according to a Reuters story ("Next For Cellphones: Nudity") reported in May 2003.

If the cellphone is indeed on its way to gobbling up the tiny portable computer and the desktop Internet, this is no doubt due not only to advantages of the cellphone but to inadequacies of the personally computed Internet. In the next chapter we examine some of the drawbacks of the Web when it reaches out to us from machines under desks and screens on tables.

Chapter 3
World Wide Spiderweb

There is something clingy in everything we see. To look at one thing is not to look at anything else. To look usefully at anything—to see with comprehension—requires a certain amount of focus and attention. Reading requires more attention than most other acts of vision, but looking at anything is a kind of careful reading, in comparison to how we hear sounds. We can listen carefully, if we choose; we can give a melody or any other sounds our undivided attention. But we also can catch music on the fly—we can entertain and be entertained by the world of sound regardless of where our heads may be turned. And this is something we cannot do with vision, which insists on our looking in the direction of the object we are regarding, and which is why radios and telephones make a lot more sense than televisions and computers for drivers of cars.

Furthermore, television requires far less attention, is far more easygoing, than most other visual activities. We can close our eyes in front of it from time to time and not be too much the worse off (unless, again, we also are driving). Certainly looking someplace else when the television is on is less rude than looking away when someone is standing or sitting right in front of us. Indeed, drifting, dozing, talking to someone in the room, just walking away while the television is on may be one of its greatest charms. It gives us time off from the more possessive, demanding activities of real life.

Television is also far less demanding than other visual media. Reading is even more monopolizing of our attention than in-person conversation. To look away from the words we are reading, even for a second, is to suspend our progress on the page; to look away any longer risks shattering it. But words printed on paper have the saving grace of being there, staying in place, exactly as we left them, when we return. This usually makes leaving them no big deal. Our progress on the page, when we look away, is usually shelved with the book, temporarily tabled with the newspaper, and we can call it back, if we like, even reconstruct it, if it has been shattered. We can put our progress on the printed page back together, unlike Humpty Dumpty, and move forward with it, the next time around.

Reading on a page on the Web offers no such security and may be the most jealous, attention-demanding activity of all. If we look away, the words on the screen may not be there when we return (plug pulled, power failure, batteries depleted). Or they may be so frozen in place that we cannot progress to the next screen (system crash). For the infinite number of screens that the Web holds out to us, it exacts this toll: we cannot look at anything off-screen too long—at least not if we want our session on the screen to remain in play. Indeed, not if we want it to remain in instant, constant recall, like the book or newspaper. Pages on computer screens can be as unreconstructable as eggshells, with crucial pieces stubbornly missing, and a good deal more perishable.

Because even if our computer and its connections are working just fine, the Web page we were reading might not be there the next time we access its URL. All pages on the Web other than our own are, after all, under the control of others, who are free to modify or delete them at any time. For that matter, even our own Web pages are not completely under our control, being at the mercy of the external computer on which the pages are stored. There is thus a world of difference between "my" Web page and "my" book—only the latter is "mine" in the sense that if I own it, nothing short of an act of nature or vandalism or theft can change that book if I do not want it changed. And if I have the book or magazine or newspaper in my physical possession, right in front of me, nothing other than those acts can keep it from me. In contrast, owning a Web page, including one that I created, is really closer to renting or borrowing it from the central computer on which it resides, since in order for the page to be displayed—even to me, on any personal computer other than my own, on which I may have filed another copy of the page—I am obliged to rent, beg, or borrow Web space on the central system.

The pages of portable books and their printed newspaper cousins are therefore less demanding, because they are more reliable, than anything on a computer screen. We are not always on the verge of losing what we see on the printed paper page. Words and pictures wedded to paper do not "tremble on the verge of disappearance"—to borrow a phrase from American philosopher John Dewey (1925, p. 148)—as do figments and pigments on the Web.

No wonder, fleeting as they are, that most transactions on the Web are done in the safety of rooms, indoors in homes or offices. We seek, of course, the more reliable electric power and telephone connection of the room inside, as well as the ease of printing out documents and Web pages indoors. There has never been much of a market for outdoor, battery-operated printers, perhaps because one big cloudburst could ruin both the paper and the printer. All of these conditions translate into the contents of our screens being more secure, less likely to escape our perusal and enjoyment, when viewed indoors. Books, newspapers, magazines, even paper notebooks and pens are made of stronger stuff. They do almost as well outdoors as indoors, they can stand up to the elements—in the instance of a book, even to a rainy day at the beach—and come home largely unscathed. Laptops and smaller computers have taken the first toddling steps outdoors. But only the cellphone can laugh at the rain and leave the room behind, without its users giving much thought to what part of its information might be lost in the great outdoors. As we will consider later, the cellphone can indeed result in a loss of information—when, for example, its ring disrupts a conversation we are having in person. But in terms of getting us out of the room, out of the building, the cellphone is usually about gain. Ladies and gentlemen, the cellphone has left the building—and you're mostly the better off for it.

Breaking Down Rooms

How did we ever get so locked into rooms? Well, they keep us warmer than winter coats in the cold, and dry in the rain, so the real question is: why do we spend so much time in rooms on beautiful days?

Electricity is to blame. Not the form of the energy itself, but the way most of it is delivered. Electricity comes through power lines, which connect to smaller conduits, which end up as outlets in the walls of our rooms. The Amish understand this distinction between electricity and its mode of delivery, and—contrary to their portrayal in popular culture—are quite happy to use electricity that flows from batteries rather than outlets in walls. This is not necessarily because the Amish prefer to be outdoors. They just do not want to be beholden to electric power companies, which are beyond their control. (They have no problem purchasing batteries manufactured and marketed by non-Amish sources, since the Amish have total control of the battery power once purchased.) The result also makes the Amish less beholden to rooms.

In the rest of the technological world, however, our big appliances—refrigerators, air conditioners, electric stoves and ovens, dishwashers—require more energy than batteries can provide. We cannot run them on the run. So we remain highly dependent on walls in rooms. The social disruption of a power failure shows how fundamental electricity in walls is to our lives. I also recall my nephew's response when, at three years of age, he and his family moved into a new home near Boston. The electricity had not yet been turned on. He was baffled and outraged—for him, electricity in walls was as natural and intrinsic to existence as sunlight coming through a window.

Most of us, though we know better intellectually, have the same gut feeling.

For almost the first fifty years of its existence, radio was a big appliance. It was "wireless" insofar as it could receive information via electromagnetic carrier waves in the air and did not require wires for that purpose, as did telephone for its communication, but a radio still had to be plugged into a wall outlet, by wire, for its electrical, operating power. Its freedom from wires for communication—not power—was nonetheless a remarkable, awe-inspiring accomplishment. Radio in effect reversed the pattern of telephone, which required wires for communication but needed less than one-fifth of a watt of direct current (power) to work. ("So faint is this power," Harry Granick pointed out, "that Bell once completed a telephone circuit through six college professors, whom he had persuaded to hold hands." See Granick's *Underneath New York*, 1947/1991, p. 132, for details on this and other fascinating telephone trivia.) Bell's invention in 1876 was essentially a mechanically powered instrument, like the phonograph invented by Edison a year later, and just a year before Edison formed his Electric Light Company, which would soon get most Americans comfortable with the idea of electrical power in the home and thus home appliances that ran on electricity.

Some two decades later, Guglielmo Marconi built the radio in the face of pronouncements by Heinrich Hertz, discoverer of electromagnetic waves, that they could never be used for practical, telecommunication purposes. Such a device would require "a mirror as large as the Continent" of Europe, pre-sumably for broadcast and/or relay purposes, Hertz had claimed (see Colin Cherry's *The Age of Access*, 1985, p. 25, for details). Hertz was laughably wrong about the literal size, and thus impossibility, of radio technology, but broadcast towers were nonetheless far too big to fit in the home. Radio thus became a one-way, highly centralizing mass medium—notwithstanding its wirelessness—unlike two-way, wired telephone. And even its one-way reception devices were at first big, immobile, and dominated most rooms.

Marconi's wireless was actually voiceless, but it was two-way—neither telephone nor radio but wireless telegraph. Reginald Fessenden in 1906 and Lee de Forest in 1907 experimented with wireless "telephony"—indeed, Bell himself had worked on a wireless "photophone," which transmitted its voices via light, rather than electricity, presaging fiber optics by a good century. But all of these experiments added up to radio—one-way wireless transmission of voices—not cellphones, at least not for another fifty years. (De Forest was also the inventor of the audion, an amplifier of telephone signals that facilitated the first long-distance telephone service in the United States in 1915.)

Hertz's and similar "never dogmatisms"—my name for the confident assertions of leading scientists and experts that such-and-such application of a technology, or utilization of a scientific discovery, can "never" occur—pepper the past two hundred years. Among its best-known appearances are the British Admiralty's pronouncement in 1828 that introduction of steam power in British warships would "strike a fatal blow at the naval supremacy of the [British] Empire," and August Comte's observation a few years later that we would never know the chemical composition of stars. "The ink was scarcely dry on [Comte's] printed page," the philosopher Charles Sanders Peirce later noted, "before the spectroscope was discovered," and provided data on the chemical makeup of distant stars via analysis of their light. Of course, we haven't actually visited any star, as yet, to corroborate such analyses, but we're just in the infancy of the space age—another possible conduit to knowledge that Comte neglected to take into account. (See William H. McNeill's *The Pursuit of Power*, 1982, p. 226, for more on steamships and war, and Peirce's "The Scientific Attitude and Fallibilism," 1896–1899, for more on the pitfalls of predicting impossibilities. I do hold that some things, such as time travel, are impossible, by the way. If we could travel to the past and prevent our grandparents from meeting, how could we later be born and travel to the past?

Such paradoxes can be resolved only by recourse to even more bizarre situations like multiple, parallel universes—one in which we are born, travel to the past, prevent our grandparents from meeting, and another universe, created by that time travel in the first universe, in which we therefore are not born. ... Such entanglements make the assessment of "impossible," or, at very least, highly unlikely, seem the most reasonable for time travel. But the perceived difficulties that lead to most "never dogmatisms" are not paradoxes, just technological shortcomings, such as inability to get to another star. Such kinds of mis-assessments seem more akin to the mis-appreciation of some technologies by their own inventors, as was the case with Edison and the phonograph, and then the motion picture, as discussed in Chapter 1—though Edison's error was not one of pessimism about his inventions, but premature optimism for certain applications.)

Speaking of impossible applications, however, it is worth noting that, as early as 1904, Rudyard Kipling captured some of the sheer cosmic verve of untethered communication in his fantastical little story "Wireless," in which a consumptive is contacted via "Hertzian waves" or Marconi wireless by the long-dead John Keats, who transmits his poetry. (" 'Tis Death is dead, not he; Mourn not for Adonais"—maybe Shelley was right, after all.) But the miracle of wireless, real or imagined, like the miracle of telephone before it, was nonetheless dispensed in rooms. Whether wires for power or wires for communication, they still all ended up in indoor outlets. Those who partook of its magic were genies in motionless bottles.

Radio later would be rescued by automobiles, batteries, and transistors, but not before its stately, stationary presence in living rooms got our parents and grandparents into the habit of thinking of electronic media as devices that lived in the home. Thus television—radio with pictures—took the looming place of radio in the living room. And the personal computer—an electric typewriter with a screen, or a television that produced text, depending on how you looked at it—stepped right up to its position on the desk.

The first desktop personal computers were much smaller than the first radios and televisions, but the desks they sat upon were not. Thus it was that when the Internet became the World Wide Web not just in name but in extent and diversity of information—in the mid-1990s—the ergonomic passport for traveling through this world was usually a chair behind an unmoving desk. Laptops allowed computing away from homes and offices, and wireless technology eventually permitted outdoor Web access, but such visits to cyberspace were carefully timed and trimmed by the duration of batteries.

The cellphone requires portable power, too, but by the late 1990s its batteries supported telephone use longer and more reliably than the Internet access provided by laptop batteries. This was in part because roaming the Web consumed more electrical energy than word processing or browsing offline and in part because Web sessions easily could last longer than cellphone conversations. The virtual infinity of possible information on the Web—the invitation of links that could lead to links that could lead to links, in effect, ad infinitum, one of the great joys and benefits of the Web—makes it a much more voracious consumer of time than the usual cellphone conversation, which concludes when either party wishes to do something else. This happens quickly, most of the time, if only because of the cellphone's tradition, especially in the United States, of both parties, caller and receiver, paying for the call. But, in addition, when the cellphone conversation takes place in public for even one of the speakers, that very fact places the speaker right in the midst of competing activities, such as eating a hotdog, running to catch a train, or just talking with someone else in person. The interjection of the cellphone into public life encourages us to mark time, to be especially aware of it, whereas the illusion of being transported to another place, cyberspace, on the Web can coax us to forget about time almost entirely. (Stationary public Web kiosks can have the same seductive effect. I once missed a train to Boston because

I was exploring the Web at the Stamford, Connecticut, station from a little terminal that was helpfully installed near the ticket booths. The same could have happened with a laptop or a Palm Pilot, but I doubt with a cellphone. Not only would the conversation likely have been shorter, but it would not have prevented me from keeping an eye on the tracks. The acoustic, again, is less possessive, less demanding of our exclusive attention than visual communication.)

Further, the laptop and the cellphone differed in their relationship to rooms from the very beginning. Although the laptop was and is used on park benches, trains, and planes—that is, out of rooms—a large part of its purpose is to allow people to take their computers from one room to another, as in office to home, home to office, home for the holidays, or from any room to outdoors, or vice versa. The laptop, in other words, was and still is rooted in a room like a plant in a pot. It sooner or later sits, and performs, somewhere in a room. It can be taken outside, and often is intended to be, but its fundamental orientation is inside. We might say laptops are special, artificial satellites that revolve around the room and inevitably come back to it (again, especially when printed copies of screen work or information are required or desired). In contrast, the cellphone was explicitly designed and intended to be used anywhere. And because its "sessions" end when its conversations end, which can be and frequently are totally outside, it has no intrinsically room-seeking orientation, no data to be copied onto the hard drive of a desktop at home or transmitted somewhere by a more reliable connection found in a room. The cellphone is thus a more intrinsically outdoor, out-of-room device than the laptop.

We probably could place all media in one of three categories regarding their "roomness," or relationship to rooms. Early radio and television, landline phones, desktop computers, movies in motion picture theaters all had or have to be in rooms, or connected to rooms by extension chords. Laptops and 45-rpm record players (popular in the 1950s, in the early days of rock 'n' roll) are transitional media regarding rooms, in that they can easily be moved from one room or home or office to another, but they usually perform in a room. Books, Kodak cameras and their progeny, car and transistor radios, portable cassette and CD players, and the cellphone take the clearest leave of rooms. Whether Frodo reading a book in the Shire on Middle Earth at the start of *The Lord of the Rings* or someone making a call from a jet plane in the air today, these roomless media work everywhere. (Books, newspapers, and magazines have the edge because they come with batteries included—any ambient light—and do not require reloading.) A book, a Sony Walkman, a cellphone are as natural to encounter outdoors as a tree, an automobile, or a bridge.

In this accounting, the Palm Pilot's access to the Internet and the Blackberry's access to e-mail—both PDAs introduced after the cellphone—can be seen as a refinement and out-growth more of the cellphone than of the laptop. Like the cellphone, the Palm Pilot and the Blackberry are explicitly intended and designed to be used out of rooms, homes, and offices. The forays for information on the Palm Pilot—such as looking for a restaurant in the area—are short and self-contained, like cellphone conversations. There is no need for a printout, because the amount of data is small enough to be readily accessible on the Palm Pilot. The same is the case for e-mail on the Blackberry and similar devices—you read and respond much as you would vocally, or in text, on the cellphone. Rooms and their printers and almost limitless power and better connections become almost irrelevant.

The benefits of spending more of our time out of rooms, outdoors, are obvious to anyone who likes fresh air, sunshine, and a snowflake or two. But, interestingly, these out-of-room media also improve life back in the room, indoors.

Spiderwebs and Bird Nests

Human beings are often hungrier for information than for food. Hence, the telephone interrupts and can trump dinner. Indeed, so irresistible is the telephone's call—it can be from anyone, including the person we most want to hear from, whether for business or pleasure, even though it is usually from a telemarketer or an in-law—that it can take precedence over anything, including lovemaking. Media theorists refer to this effect as "telephonus interruptus."

Until the cellphone, the telephone was even more inextricably indoors than big-appliance media. This was not because it required large amounts of electricity for power, but because electricity served as the conduit of information. Like the telegraph before it, the telephone conveys via electrical patterns—encodings or transformations of voices and sounds—and this, until the cellphone, required wires. (Cordless phones, in widespread use at least a decade before cellphones, allowed people to walk around the house, and even step right outdoors, while on the phone. But they couldn't move much farther than that, away from the phone's base in the home. Still, the cordless phone can be considered one of the first fledgling steps toward the cellphone.)

Indeed, one of the big innovations and advantages of the telephone compared to the telegraph was that the phone brought wires and thus the ability to communicate long distance directly into the home. But once thus ensconced in wires, no battery alone could liberate the phone—batteries provided only power, no electronic encodings of conversation. For those who wanted to make or receive phone calls outside of the home or office, a phone situated in a specially constructed little cubicle, with wires—the public phone, in a booth—was the only option. In New York City in the 1960s and 1970s, the last decades prior to the cellphone, public phone booths on some street corners reeked so regularly of urine that the phone company tore down the booths and left just the phone on a stalk. Unfortunately, this let in not only sunshine but car honks and exhaust fumes. The conditions of attendance—the circumstances in which we utilize a medium—were not greatly improved.

But the convenience of having the world at hand at home via the phone also had its cost, as we have seen—there was no easy way of shutting the world off, other than pulling the phone out of the wall. When the world was unwanted—when the phone call was an intrusion, an irritation, a disruption of the peace and sanctity of our home or of whatever activity we chose to pursue there—the wire was the snake in our Garden of Eden, and the telephone its sweet-and-sharp-tongued head. Seen in this light, every intrusion of a cellphone call in a restaurant today could be one less intrusion of a phone call at home (if not one less call in an office, which may not be intrusive). Somewhere in this calculus of intrusions in which we want, in part, to keep business calls in places of business, the cellphone provides a net benefit for rooms at home. It lures the snake out of the house and siphons off some of its hiss.

Even when business is not the purpose of the call—even for media like the Internet, which offer much more than phone conversations—what is the advantage of having all media, all acts of communication, crowded into the nest at home? It's certainly good to have opportunities for communication in easy reach, to be able to avail ourselves of all media services whenever we please, including when we are home, which for many of us is most or a lot of the time. But the telephone is in a class of its own when it comes to announcing itself. It rings of its own volition, not ours, and in effect pages us, programs us, literally calls on us and call us forth, rather than vice versa. Might not the home be more enjoyable with a bit less of such self-initiating communication? Televisions do not usually turn themselves on, unless we have programmed them to do so, for all that their supposedly disruptive effect on the family has been lamented. We may curse the radio alarm clock, but we are the ones who set it. That disrupter of sleep, that shatterer of a last sweet dream, is doing our bidding, much as we might not like it. But even regarding radio that we do want to hear, every bit of it heard outside the home is one less sound we hear in the home, in competition with voices of loved ones and friends. Every session on the Web we spend at home is an excursion into cyberspace at the expense of family space.

Access to the Web on mobile devices outside the home thus not only frees us from the sticky spiderweb of seat and screen, but makes the home nest more convivial. The growing availability of media outside the home, not only in libraries and cyber-cafés but in cars and pockets, makes each of us a nest or hearth of communications—a hearth we can explore and enjoy without clipping or short-circuiting the hearth at home.

In the next chapter we explore some of the advantages of cellphones and the mobile hearths they are creating—some of the benefits of communicating outside.

Chapter 4
The Mobile Hearth

John Culkin (1915–1993), early disciple of Marshall McLuhan, former Jesuit and professor at Fordham University, loved to talk about the four words pertinent to communication embedded in "hearth": hear, heart, ear, earth. These words are especially applicable to the cellphone—not quite come of age in John Culkin's time—and its reach.

Human beings were mobile hearths of communication prior to the cellphone, indeed, from the moment we and our brains first appeared on this Earth. We hear, see, talk, walk, jump, think, feel, dream, all coordinated and processed through our command center on feet—our brain. But our multitasking communications were all short distance. Prior to technology, our ability to communicate was limited by the biological boundaries of eyesight and earshot, the strength of our legs to stretch and shift these boundaries, the tenuous capacity of our memories to save information for a time when the boundaries shifted, because our legs moved, to allow us to communicate. I call this long dawn of human communication—of humanity— Stage A, a realm of maximum, literally full-bodied communication, but all at short range, and spiced throughout by wild, unimplementable imagination. (See my "Human Replay," 1979, and *The Soft Edge*, 1997, for more.) It was thus at once a very real, point-blank, what-you-see-is-what-you-get realm, and a place of always tempting, unattainable magic, where the mind's eye and ear brought us images and sounds from far away, long ago, that we could never actually see or hear. It lasted until carving, scribbling, drawing, writing finally enabled us, for the first time, actually to send information, in forms much less perishable than memories, to faraway places and to the future, where they could be retrieved by other humans.

This installation of early technologies—Stage B—was a trade-off, or progress at a cost: writing indeed may have been the voice of an absent person, as Freud aptly observed in *Civilization and Its Discontents* (1930/1961), but the written voice of the alphabet had neither sound nor face. It was, as McLuhan remarked in *The Gutenberg Galaxy* (1962), "neutral." And not only maddeningly, but gladdeningly so, for the words looked like, sounded like, nothing and therefore could easily represent anything and everything, including, even, nothing. This ease of extensive representation included things that were not physically present, things that never had any physical existence in the first place—things such as ideas and concepts, including the concept of concept and the concept of nothing. (Is there anything about the literal look and sound of the combined letters "m," "a," and "d" that seem angry, or anything about the letters "g," "l," "a," and "d" that are happy? They could just as easily mean precisely the reverse, or something completely unrelated to anger or joy.)

Millennia later, Morse's telegraph went even further, in both pros and cons, giving us instant transmission of writing across vast distances, but in a form—Morse code—that required special decoding to read. Morse code was an abstraction of the written word, which was in turn an abstraction of the spoken word, which was in turn once removed from reality. (Do the spoken words "dog" or "cow" have any real connection to the animals they describe? The onomatopoetic "bark" and "moo" do—they sound a bit like what they denote—but they are minor, trivial examples in our language.) The speed of telegraph transmission thus could be received only in a seat that was three rows back from reality, with lots of hats and big heads in between.

The telegraph was the high point and heyday of trade-offs, the maximum sacrifice of reality for speed of communication. The next stage of media evolution—Stage C, the final stage—would make available to us all information, real images and sounds, as well as abstract words, anyplace we might be, any time we chose. We have not completely settled in there as yet. But we have had a foot in the door since the photograph, developed at the same time—mostly the second two decades of the nineteenth century—as the telegraph, and almost by the same man. Samuel Morse traveled to Paris in 1838–1839 to introduce his telegraph to the French. He ran into L. J. M. Daguerre that winter, and saw his photographic plates—"daguerreotypes." Morse wrote back to his brothers in New York City in March 1839: "You may recall experiments of mine in New Haven (Yale College) many years ago . . . experiments to ascertain whether it were possible to fix the images of the camera obscura. . . . [B]ut finding that light produced dark, and dark light, I presumed the production of a true image to be impracticable and gave up the attempt. M. Daguerre has realized in the most exquisite manner this idea." (See Josef Maria Eder, *History of Photography*, 1945/1978, pp. 272–73 for more.)

The photograph gave us at least a part of reality exactly as it was, in contrast to paintings filtered through the talent of artists and written descriptions even more removed from the world. But the part of reality in the first photographs was narrow—still, silent, black-and-white, two-dimensional. Successive improvements in photography—the introduction of motion, sound, color, and even the third dimension, in holography, in the late 1940s—broadened and deepened the photographic rendition of reality, and brought us more fully into Stage C. They kicked the door wide open, at least insofar as our capacity to view images captured of people and the world.

But the installation of communication technologies in the home during these years—making the home a communication hearth—was a Stage B trade-off of a different kind. On the one hand, we got greater pieces of reality piped right into the home. Telephone gave us long-distance conversation in the home, moving us two big rows closer to reality, ahead of telegraph and letter writing, when we wanted to communicate with people far away or indeed anywhere beyond our physical presence. Radio moved us to the front row, too, certainly in comparison to the newspaper as a vehicle of news; and television gave us an even better view from this row, with images as well as sounds. But the home became packed with all manner of media, while outside we remained mostly deprived, limited in our range by biology, multitaskers without long-range portfolio.

The revolution in mobile media, when books began to move incisions from walls, had actually been changing this aspect of Stage B millennia before photography naturalized the image. Kodak cameras, radios, and now cellphones have brought this adjustment, this refinement of media progress, into full swing. We stand now, with a cellphone and its voices, sounds, images, and written words in hand on instant command, on the full veranda of Stage C. But the new light is bright, even blinding, and we cannot yet clearly see all that awaits us out there.

What are its most profound benefits?

Instantly Implemented Imagination

Well, not quite. We can imagine far more than possibly can be implemented by any cellphone, indeed any technology—for instance, time travel, or being physically in more than one place at the same time (in contrast to virtually, in cyberspatial or other kinds of electronic copies, which is easy). Nonetheless . . .

The cellphone is currently the epitome of mobility in media because it allows both reception (like the book and the transistor radio) and production (like the Kodak camera), allows this immediately and long distance (like the transistor radio), and allows this interactively (like no prior mobile medium). The result of all of these capacities instantly at hand is that the contents of our minds, including ideas, impulses, strategies, become a fingertip away from implementation.

In a world of omni-communication, thoughts and ideas are easier to enact.

Prior to the cellphone, homes and offices were the sites of most media enactments. Motion picture theaters, phone booths, and early mobile devices provided exceptions, but these external media occasions usually permitted just one kind of communication transaction—watching a movie, talking on the phone, listening to the radio. (Face-to-face interpersonal communication—conversation—took place everywhere, just as readily outside as inside homes and offices, and entailed seeing, hearing, and potentially touching.) The cellphone began as a strictly one-dimensional medium, too—a miniaturized phone booth that could be carried in a baggy pocket or pocketbook. Like the phone booth, all the cellphone could do was convey spoken conversation. But as soon as the cellphone began hooking into the Internet or offering some of its features—books, newspapers, magazines, live and delayed conversation in text, telephone, videophone, radio, music recordings, photographs, television—the cellphone became a home away from home for communications, a mobile home or pocket hearth, a traveling medium of media.

What will result from having most of the continuum of possible communication at our fingertips? We began as a species with communication at fingertip impulse, but only for communication very close at hand. We progressed to a life in which the impulse to communicate with people and about things far away could be gratified, but not completely, and only immediately if we were at home or in another suitable indoor place. Otherwise, the gratification was delayed until we physically arrived at such a place. The cellphone gives us that gratification just about anywhere, wherever we may be, with no need for delay.

Instant gratification has something of a bad reputation in our culture. Its pursuit is said to be childish, a sign that an individual has not achieved an adult maturity, an emotional understanding and acceptance that things in life take time.

Technologies ranging from television and its fast information to fast food to psychedelic drugs have thus all been herded under the contemptible umbrella of instant gratification and its alleged destructiveness. But the situation is far more complicated, at least in regard to immediate gratification in communication.

Responding in the heat of anger is, admittedly, not usually a good idea. "Flaming" in e-mail, instant messaging, and more public online places—replying more acrimoniously than one might in person or on the telephone—usually does no one a service and is certainly one of the drawbacks of online discussion. It is likely facilitated by the parties not seeing each others' faces or hearing their voices, which removes various cues that might reduce misunderstanding, and also emboldens harsh responses: it's easier to be aggressive to a screen than a face. Also, being online late at night, at home, in usually private surroundings, encourages responses that are private—for example, what we really think of a person—even though these responses are publicly communicated and viewable by who-knows-who on message boards, listserves, and chat rooms. (Several message boards that I have read and posted on have special topics called "Flames." The moderator of the message board moves postings that are highly offensive or that traffic in insult and name-calling from general topics down to "Flames." This serves the dual purpose of removing them from general discussions and providing a specific place where all of them can be read, for those online readers who enjoy the online bread-and-circus of flaming.)

But what about conveying an apology? Isn't a cellphone in hand preferable to letting the discord fester? And in what way is anything to be gained by not being able to consult a dictionary or encyclopedia or movie review on impulse, or not being able to say "Hi, I arrived safe and sound" as soon as possible? (I guess consulting a movie review with which you might not agree—thereby steering you toward a movie you dislike or away from a movie you would love—is no advantage. Okay, then, subtract that from the undeniable benefits. But that still leaves correct spelling, facts at hand, and comfort to friends and loved ones.)

Urban planner Lewis Mumford (1895–1990) was highly critical of most twentieth-century technology and thought that delay, separation of thought and action, was absolutely necessary for rational decision. He worried that radio, the big, immediate medium in the first half of his life, would flood society with information that—unlike the text of newspapers and magazines—was gone the instant it was spoken and therefore was unavailable for careful examination and re-examination. (Mumford was an interesting contrast to Socrates, who worried that the inertness, noninteractivity, of writing made it a danger and dagger to the intellect.) Mumford feared that instant radio would encourage hasty, emotional judgments and responses, which would undermine the democratic process (already jeopardized by an uninformed electorate, as decried by Walter Lippmann in his *Phantom Public*, in 1922). Mumford's qualms certainly were realized in Adolf Hitler, whose radio addresses galvanized the German people. Hitler had earlier written in *Mein Kampf* (1924/1971) that he distrusted newspaper journalists, because they interpreted rather than reported his views—or, actually, *because* they reported his views, which he wanted to present to the German people directly, without the mediation of the press.

But radio also enabled Joseph Stalin to inspire the Soviet people and their "scorched earth" policy, which helped stop the Nazi conquest of their country. And the democratic leaders Winston Churchill and Franklin Roosevelt also used radio to great advantage. (See Chapter 8, "Radio Heads," of my book *The Soft Edge*, 1997, for more.) The wielding of radio on behalf of freedom suggests that there is nothing inherently totalitarian—or irrational—in immediate information. Or, if instant information is effective in quickly mobilizing mass opinion, there is no reason that such opinion need be irrational and its application nondemocratic. Surely our logic, as well as our emotion, can be lightning quick, as when we suddenly see a completely rational solution to a problem. And while Churchill and Roosevelt were no doubt strong leaders, and their strength was facilitated by a capacity to talk to their people directly by radio, their tenures left the democratic process vigorously intact—indeed, so much so that Churchill's party lost the election in the United Kingdom after World War II. (Even FDR's Democratic Party was voted out of office in 1952, when Republican Dwight David Eisenhower easily beat Democrat Adlai Stevenson.)

But if immediacy in media cuts both ways, the cut no doubt goes to the very bone of tradition. The mere word "immediate"—"im," or the negation of, "mediate"—shows how contrary immediate communication is to what we expect of media. We converse with people in our immediate surroundings, immediately; we converse with people not in our immediate vicinity via media, and that takes, or should take, time. But is that expectation anything more than a reflection of past circumstances and their inadequacies?

In a world in which writing was the only game of long-distance communication in town (and country), delay was ubiquitous, impossible to evade. After the invention of the telephone, the delay was for as long as it took us to reach a place—a house, an office, a hallway, a street corner—with phone. The same was true of radio (less so, once radio moved into cars and then out onto the sidewalks via transistors) and television (more so, since television was mostly available in homes, and in some windows of big department stores in the early days, but never, literally, on streets or street corners) and the desktop Internet (probably initially about the same as television, with libraries substituting for department store windows). But today the cellphone is heating up and rapidly evaporating those last puddles of delay. When the cellphone has completely permeated our society, when immediacy in media is the de facto order of the day, there will no longer be any contradiction between immediate and media, no whiff of oxymoron. At that point, media and immediate will be one and the same.

Of course, we have not quite reached that point yet. Only two-thirds of the adult population in the United States, 140 to 150 million people, subscribed to cellular service in 2002, and although that number is an extraordinary 41,000 percent increase over the 340,000 subscribers in 1985 (the first year statistics on cellphone subscribers were gathered) and will certainly continue to grow by leaps and bounds, the cellphones such subscribers use are still prone to far more busy signals, busy circuits, outages of range, and like obstacles than conventional landline phones. But these are technicalities— shortcomings in technology that come from its being in its infancy or early childhood. We ought not assess the range of the butterfly on the basis of the caterpillar. Indeed, the beautiful orange-and-black Monarch butterfly soars from New England and New York to Mexico, while its striped caterpillar crawls just a few inches on milkweed plants far below. When the cellphone has been around as long as the butterfly—or just the book, or even the in-place telephone— the world will be very different from what it is today.

The Telepathic Society

The immediacy of one-way mass media such as radio and tele- vision allowed us to receive but not send information any time we wanted, as long as we were in the right place. But the infor- mation was usually rehearsed, programmed, performed—in a word, public, not private. The great illusion of all mass media—be they books, radio, or television—is that their mes- sages, crafted for no one person in particular, are meant to *feel* for all the world as if they were intended for each of us. The newscaster looks directly into a camera when she is speaking on her set. At home, I look at my screen and can almost believe she is talking to me. If, as Samuel Coleridge held in his 1817

(1907) *Biographia Literaria*, a "willing suspension of disbelief" was necessary for appreciation of poetry, it is also a prerequisite for the effective operation of all mass media.

In contrast, the one-to-one conversations of telephones in homes, offices, and booths required no such suspensions or illusions. Both parties were truly talking to one another. Unlike the radio listener, whose personal connection to the radio voice is passive and imaginary, the telephone listener's connection to the voice at the other end of the line is active, interactive, interchangable (the listener can become the speaker, and vice versa), and real. Twenty-five years prior to the advent of radio and electronic mass media, the telephone thus allowed us to speak our minds instantly, and initiated the (indoor) telepathic society.

Note that this kind of telephonic telepathy entails *speaking* of minds, not reading of minds. We convey our thoughts through speech on the phone and thus can choose what we want to say and convey. We can choose to say nothing. Our innermost privacy thus remains within our control in any telephone conversation, landline or cellular. The telepathic society is thus ultimately not about invasion of privacy, and is quite different from David Brin's (1998) "transparent society," a world in which we have no secrets.

But depending on whom we were talking to, the phone booth could put more pressure on our privacy than the sights and sounds of the outside world. Indeed, if we are talking to anyone on the phone, whether at home or in public, chances are that person means more to us than just about anyone else we might encounter outdoors. And the cellphone has transformed every pocket and handbag and therefore the whole world into a huge phone booth. This whole-world-as-phone-booth is every bit as big as the world prior to cellphones—even bigger, because it comes with the possibility of access to anyone, anytime. But this world is not stuffy and cramped like the phone booth—it consists physically of the whole wide world, and the space station, too. So, no, it is not cramped—that is, unless you find that being accessible all the time cramps your style. (The cellphone and whole-world-as-phone-booth also have undercut the need for the traditional phone booth and the public phone in the sunshine, which has been withering on its metal stalks. A colleague told me a story of a friend of hers, a young woman, recently locked out of her building without her key. She asked a passerby if she could borrow a quarter to use a pay phone to call her friend—my informant—who had a copy of the key and lived nearby. The passerby gave the young woman a quizzical look and offered her the use of his cellphone.) (See also the 2003 movie *Phone Booth*, a terrifying, savvy elegy for the departing booth.)

We can only guess about how this new world will change our lives. How different are we from Victorians prior to the telephone, whose tidings from afar, news, business, and personal, came on paper, usually taking days, rarely hours, almost never minutes? (Pneumatic tubes first used for delivery of telegrams from the Central Telegraph Company to the Stock Exchange in London in 1853 were the exception. They were improved and installed in many big cities in ensuing decades, carried mail as well as telegrams, and eventually could move such printed materials more than thirty miles per hour. But by then an increasing amount of business and personal communication was conducted vocally, on the phone, which began to eat into the long-distance monopoly of paper.) The homes of pre-phone Victorians were truly castles, difficult to penetrate, at least insofar as communication, whatever their construction and decoration. But not only their homes were impervious to immediate long-range communication. Their very bodies, their skins, their selves were protected, insulated, isolated, wherever they traveled. To be on the road, any road, was to be incommunicado in those days, beyond any talking except from someone walking or otherwise moving alongside of you.

These people and their predecessors wrote words we can readily understand, words about communication. They were Shakespeare, saying all the world's a stage; Jefferson, commenting that given a choice between a world of government and no press, or press and no government, he would choose the latter (see Jefferson's letter 1802 to the Comte de Volney, discussed in Emery and Emery, 1992, p. 74); and Coleridge on the willing suspension of disbelief. So their media and circumstances of communication did not make them utterly or even mostly alien to us. Indeed, they thought about communication, probed and sought to understand its impact, much as we do. We thus can well understand even what Socrates said through Plato's writing in the *Phaedrus* more than two thousand years earlier about the inadequacy of writing—unlike conversation, it is fixed, unvarying, not immediately responsive—and now recognize how writing via the Internet and the cellphone remedies this limitation of the written word. (See my "Intelligent Writing: The Electronic Liberation of Text," 1989, for more on this fulfillment of the Socratic ideal for writing.)

So the telepathic society that we are now bringing into being via the cellphone should be no less recognizable to us than our recent world would have been to Socrates and Jefferson. Indeed, Socrates might well have felt especially comfortable in this new telepathic world, seeing as how it maximizes the opportunity for dialog, which he so valued. And Jefferson, disputer of big government, champion of individual expression nurtured by maximum information, might well have felt the same.

The clearest prediction that I think can be made about a cellphone with Internet access in everyone's pocket is that it will strengthen the self in its voyage through the world. Put more directly: We and our descendants will be able to do more of what we want to do, be it business or pleasure, pursuit of knowledge, details, companionship, love. We will be able to accomplish more of this, because we will be able to reach the people and places that have this information much faster and more easily than at any time in the past. Indeed, place will become far less relevant as a source of information than it is today, because we will be able to reach anyone, regardless of the places they and we may be. And this in turn will allow each of us to be in many more places than in the past, because all places will be the same as far as their access to everyone else's face and voice and the world's stored information. This will be not quite what Joshua Meyrowitz had in mind in his 1985 *No Sense of Place*. Instead, rather than our sense of place disappearing, it will be everywhere.

More than intelligent buildings and automobiles, we will all have, by virtue of our cellphones, intelligent pockets and smart hands. And thus, at least insofar as their capacity to support interactive communication and provide extensive off-site information, every place in the world in which a human may choose to tread will be well-read, or "intelligent." The cellphone with its Internet connections will smarten the world. This represents an interesting extension, even reversal, of the previous situation in which we, the visitors, might get smarter by walking through a given part of the world. Now that part of the world itself gets smarter, by virtue of our visit, since we bring to that place access to all other information via the cellphone, and make ourselves reachable in that place by others not in that place, besides.

Of course, we won't have access to any more touch or physical presence in the telepathic society than we have today. Telepathy, after all, is not teleportation. We'll be able to see anyone's face via videophone, wherever they are, if they so choose, but we won't be able to stroke and kiss it, unless the person not only so chooses but is standing or sitting or reclining right next to us. The telepathic society, in other words, will be all about nonmaterial information, and therefore unrequited touch.

But, both despite and because of all of these vastly increased opportunities for access to information and people, our progress as individuals in the telepathic society will be tough going at times. The ability of everyone to express the impulse to communicate instantly means that not only can we do this vis-à-vis everyone else in the world, but everyone else in the world can reach, or attempt to reach, us.

In subsequent chapters we consider some of these burdens of cellphones and the telepathic society, and what we can do to mitigate, work around, and otherwise control them.

Chapter 5
The Drawbacks of Always Being in Touch

Back in ancient 1976, a century after the invention of the telephone, Marshall McLuhan remarked that the automobile was the last place a North American could be alone. He was talking not only about a driver with no passengers, but, more important, about homes that had been breached by telephone calls for a hundred years. His observation was both keenly insightful and flavored with a dash of hyperbole, like most of McLuhan's announcements. There were many paths in parks and mountainsides where people could be alone, or close to it, though a car speeding at 60 mph did make the driver less approachable than anyone on foot. But by the end of the twentieth century, that distinction no longer mattered: The cellphone has left us no place to be alone, whether car or park or mountaintop.

The advent of the telephone made being out of touch a fine art. In prior times, it was a nearly ubiquitous fact of life. As the twentieth century progressed, secretaries became increasingly schooled in saying that their bosses were not in, when they were standing right next to the secretary's desk. Spouses provided the same service for each other at home. If I had to identify the lie that I have most committed in my adulthood, it probably would be asking my wife to tell a caller I was not at home, or doing the same favor for her. (But, not to worry, if you're reading this and you know me, I would certainly never do that to *you!*) Even children are pressed into service on behalf of such white lies for their parents.

But the cellphone, alas, shifts the burden from secretary or spouse or other family member to yourself: You are by far the most likely person to be answering your cellphone, no one else. This unavoidable fact has given rise to various strategies of avoidance, ranging from shutting the cellphone off to just letting it ring, unanswered. In most cases the strategies include claiming that you did not hear the ring, had no idea the cellphone was off, or insisting that indeed the cellphone was not off (and that your caller got a mistaken indication that it was off—nothing like offense as the best defense).

Usually unexamined in these strategies of avoidance is just why we need to deny or conceal the fact that we don't want to talk at that moment. Why has freedom of *non*-expression become such a struggle?

Consolations for the Hermit

The basic problem with declining to talk at a given moment is that, absent a suitably compelling reason—you're late to pick up your grandmother, who is standing on a corner on a busy intersection waiting for you on a rainy day—such refusal of communication seems rude. Perhaps this view has roots in times past when communication with anyone not at hand was so difficult— hey, I managed to expend all of this effort to send you a letter, a telegram, reach you on this crackly phone, now the least you can do is respond. Certainly daily floods of unbidden e-mails these days make them easy to ignore, in contrast to their slow, even rare, beginnings in the 1980s, when receipt of an e-mail had an air of adventure, an aura of thrill and satisfaction that you and the sender had both made it to the promised digital land. I remember the first e-mail I ever received, from Langdon Winner, media critic (author of *Autonomous Technology*), in reply to an e-mail I had sent to him—the first e-mail I had ever sent—shortly after logging on to the Electronic Information Exchange System (EIES, an early online system running on a minicomputer located at the New Jersey Institute of Technology in Newark), and discovering he had an account there. I was delighted! "I got a response from Langdon!" I shouted out to my wife, who came running in to see it. That was in June 1984.

But as we continue to move from scarcity to abundance of communication, the welcome breakthrough becomes an annoyance. Information underload becomes overload, which in turn becomes a different kind of underload, as we look doggedly for strategies, information, to help us navigate, cope with, the new abundance. This approach works. We walk into a library or bookstore and see many more books than we could possibly read in a lifetime, let alone choose to borrow or buy at that moment, and yet we do not feel overwhelmed very long, if at all. Why not? Because we have learned, since childhood, roughly where books are shelved in libraries and bookstores. We know fiction is in one section, nonfiction in another, biographies in yet a third. And we know, further, that fiction and nonfiction are shelved in categories (science fiction, history), with books in each category in alphabetic order of the authors' last names, and biography in alphabetic order of the subjects' last names. We know all of these rules of engagement and thus feel no more than a twinge or two of anxiety, if even that, when we encounter vast rooms of books.

Search engines on the Web, most prominently Google in 2003, serve a similar purpose. Indeed, the Web would not be usable—or not usable the way it is today—were it not for search engines. So, the Dewey decimal shelving system in libraries and search engines on the Internet are the critically important additional packets of information that we need to make the most out of the myriad of paper books and online pages available to us. But we have yet to develop and disseminate a proper operating manual for life on the lineless cellphone. Until then, the hermit can be an admirable, maybe a model, citizen for some of us, or most of us sometimes.

Where do we begin our trip back to civilization? The first step in dealing with the avalanche of accessibility that awaits us, I think, is recognizing that refusal to communicate is a reasonable option, and need not be insulting. Freedom to communicate—what the mobile hearth of the cellphone provides—surely includes the freedom not to communicate. Indeed, in a world in which we were constantly in communication with everyone, whether we wanted to be or not, the act of communicating would become almost meaningless. If we had no choice but to communicate, all the time, then communication would lose the significance of being a positive, deliberate act, a special attention to bestow. It would be less human in that sense, less an expression of free will and more a reflex than even eating, since we always can choose not to eat, at least for a short time. We can even hold our breath, for a minute or two.

But that world of undeniable, ubiquitous communication could never come into being in the first place. We cannot communicate all the time with everyone, because to communicate with just one person, to have a simple, two-way conversation, is not to communicate in that way at that moment with anyone else. So it turns out that the act of communication intrinsically entails choices—not only whether to communicate or not, but if we do decide to communicate with someone, whom are we therefore deciding not to communicate with at that time?

But given this inescapable logic of avoidance, how do we implement it in actual cellphonic practice? We can begin with not overly worrying about offending when we're not available to talk. And we can look for new customs to support refusals to communicate, as more of the world becomes accessible twenty-four hours a day.

Customs of Refusal

Refusals of communication are not new to society. "Do not disturb" signs on hotel doors mean don't even knock and ask me if I want my room to be cleaned, I don't want to talk to anyone about that or anything else right now. And we need no signs of any kind to know not to call people after their bedtime.

Laws are the ultimate way of regulating our communication, or any activity, but the heavy hand of the law is indeed a heavy-handed way of molding behavior. In February 2003 the New York City Council overrode the mayor's veto and banned the use of cellphones in Broadway theaters and movie houses, and, just for good measure, in museums, libraries, and galleries. (Sports events were exempted.) Mayor Michael Bloomberg expressed his opposition thusly: "We do not hesitate to 'shush'. . . . Some standards of conduct, not directly affecting public health or safety, can best be enforced not through legislation but through less formal means."

A good point, indeed. What's next? Should we outlaw snoring during public performances? Should we fine the people who always seem to sit right in back of me in movie theaters and offer ongoing commentary? (The penalty for violating the cellphone law is $50.) I do admit that at the beginning of every class I teach, I explain to the students that dozing off is okay, as long as they don't snore and drown out my lecture. . . . (But even so, I would never actually formally penalize—downgrade—students for snoring. Hey, if they miss my scintillating lecture, I figure that's penalty enough.)

The laws in some states against handheld cellphone use by drivers are, of course, a different matter, and may be necessary, because the stakes with a distracted driver could be life and death. And there are far fewer potential "shushers" for the cellphonic driver than the moviegoer—just whoever else might be in the car at the time, which could be no one. But the more general revolution of communication refusal will require less stern stuff.

Electing not to own a cellphone at all is the most effective way of avoiding unwanted calls—unwanted whether by you or your audience. But this means no desired calls can be received, either, not to mention not being able to make calls. There have been people who have said no, famously and anonymously, to one or more new media over the years. Lewis Mumford was concerned not only about radio and the immediacy of the information it delivered. He is said to have banned television outright from his home in Amenia, New York. Harlan Ellison and Gore Vidal are writers who claimed to eschew the personal computer in the 1980s. And the Amish, as noted in Chapter 3, refuse all technologies that require connection to central power or wires in the home, including television and telephone. But the Amish use cellphones and laptop computers that run on batteries, and some Amish have phone shacks on the edges of their property. (See my "The Amish Get Wired—The Amish?" 1993, for more.) Even before the cellphone, the telephone was an especially difficult medium to refuse, since, unlike the television, it conveys the live voices of friends, relatives, and business associates.

The Amish are significant on this question of refusal for another reason: media are easier to refuse when the denial is adopted by a group of mutually supporting people, rather than disparate individuals. Short of cellphonic anonymous withdrawal groups, there is little likelihood of that happening with the cellphone. The pressure is all the other way, toward adoption, which is self-perpetuating: Every new owner of a cellphone wants to validate that decision by being able to talk to friends, relatives, and business associates at times of the caller's choosing, which can best be accommodated when the people intended to receive the calls also have cellphones. Individuals can hold out, ironically, to the extent that they do not have social connections—have no loved ones not at home, no personal or business acquaintances—since the expectation and increasing prerequisite of those relationships in the current world is to be reachable via cellphone. Indeed, lack of a cellphone can make more difficult not only social relationships, but basic acts of life like eating, which can be facilitated by a call from a car to a take-out restaurant. The self-sufficient hermit, who needs nothing more from the outside world in companionship or nutrition, nothing more of anything, is for better or worse actually becoming the only viable alternative in a world in which everyone else is connected.

But precisely because it takes two to tango with two-way media such as telephone, the attainment of a critical mass—a state in which it is socially debilitating not to have one—seems to proceed at a much slower rate, at first, than for one-way media such as television. The telephone, as mentioned earlier, took seventy-five years to appear in more than 50 percent of American homes, and the first mobile phones were available in the cars of the rich as early as the 1950s. In contrast, television was practically universal in American homes within ten years after its commercial introduction in the late 1940s, and the personal computer (primarily a one-way medium, other than its use for e-mail) introduced in the form of Apples, CP/M machines, and IBM PCs and clones in the early 1980s, surpassed the 50 percent mark within two decades. The reason for such rapid acceptance is that you can benefit from a television, a computer, an older one-way medium such as a book, even if you're all alone, with no social interest or skills, in the middle of the night. (As discussed in Chapter 2, however, a personal computer does take significantly more technical skill to operate than television or telephone, and on that score the latter two media have more in common with each other than does either with the computer.) A one-way mass medium— ironic, in view of its "mass" distribution of information— requires only individual, single, unconnected consumers (that is, unconnected to one another) to work, unlike any two-way interpersonal medium.

But, on the other side of the curve, once critical mass for a two-way medium such as telephone is achieved, social penalties for its lack of adoption seem much more severe than for one-way media. I conduct a little experiment in my "Introduction to Mass Media" undergraduate courses, which I have been teaching under one title or another for more than a quarter century. If I were the Devil, I tell my students, and I was going to take away all of your media, except for one, which medium would you not want to part with? Television, radio (because of its music), and personal computers usually get a few votes. Telephone wins by a landslide every term. Of course it does. Few people would value possible conversation with a loved one or someone who could hire you for a sought-after job less than an image or voice speaking not really to you but to a camera or microphone. And recently, when I distin-guish between landline phones and cellphones, the victor is increasingly the cellphone. (Some astute students also know that phone calls can be made through some Internet connec-tions, and choose the Internet as a way of having both the Web and the phone, not to mention online radio.)

The coalescing of a growing, worldwide cellphone commu-nity also works against the safeguard of cellphone numbers not being publicly available. An individual who has a cell-phone and refuses to divulge its number to a friend or associ-ate who requests it does so at the risk of damaging that relationship. Lying altogether about having a cellphone might be preferable, except such a lie would be exposed the first time the cellphone rang with a call from someone who did have the number, and the person lied to was present. Individuals of course could have silent rings on their phones, but an urgent call still would require the recipient to part company with the deluded associate and find a place to receive or return the call, much like Clark Kent running into a phone booth to change into Superman. Except in the case of the cellphone, the booth would be in the recipient's pocket, and the telephone and its conversation would be the very object of the heroic exercise.

The upshot of this for cellphone numbers is that they will likely be publicly available anyway before too long. No charges for received calls is a first step. (Costs of receiving calls was the initial reason the numbers were unpublished.) By 2003 global cellphone number directories were already available on the Web. Also in 2003, cellphone numbers became transferable from phone to phone, including landline to cellphone. In an interview with *The Christian Science Monitor* (Lamb, 2003), I noted that our cellphone number may be on its way to replacing our social security number as our personal ID—except our cellphone number would be an "intelligent" social security number, capable not only of identifying us but enabling people to call us.

The gist of this explosion in accessibility is that, as we move more fully into the telepathic society, we will have to rely on individual decisions to say no—not to cellphone use entirely (for soon everyone who has a telephone will also have a cellphone, or will replace the landline phone with a cellphone), not even to the divulging of cellphone numbers (for soon these will be as available as traditional telephone numbers), but to responding, acknowledging, or allowing receipt of a call at a given time.

Just as we need not respond to written correspondence immediately, just as we are learning to do that with e-mail—to select the e-mail in need of immediate response—so we will do the same with cellphone calls. Of course, written letters and even e-mail have a built-in delay. They are asynchronous, not immediately interactive, and even though e-mail can be received immediately after it is sent, it does not fetch us, literally call out to us and request response, like a ringing phone. So protocols of avoidance and delay will be more difficult to design and enforce for the cellphone. (Some e-mail programs do emit sounds when a new e-mail is received. But the computer has to be on, and we usually need to be in the same room to hear the sound. On the other hand, a text message on the cellphone is like a phone call.) But to the degree that our intrinsic need for privacy and control over our communication, our human tempos, require such time-outs, we will carve them into our social expectations. And, as more of us do that, the more that such self-regulation of cellphone accessibility will become the social norm. The same increase in numbers that drives cellphone use thus will drive and implement expectations that all users will be out of touch at times of their choosing.

This eventual fallback in the amount of rings and public conversations also should help with the "audience" drawback of the cellphone, which arises when its use disturbs people other than the cellphone user, as in movie theaters and public performances of plays. Last year, a cellphone rang during a eulogy at a funeral I was attending. I didn't really mind it because I knew it would provide material for at least a line or two in this book, and I guess I wasn't all that close to the deceased. Others in the room felt very differently. More recently, a cellphone rang—playing "Take Me Out to the Ballgame"—during Andrew Postman's moving eulogy to his father, Neil (to whom this book is dedicated; Neil Postman was my doctoral mentor, and the closest I had to an intellectual father). Andrew and most of the mourners took the interruption in good cheer. First, it validated Neil's critique of technology. Second, Neil loved baseball. But no amount of reduction in the amount of time we talk on the cellphone could eliminate this problem completely, unless we elected to use the cellphone only in completely private places, which also would eliminate one of its most important advantages.

In the next chapter, we give full attention to the cellphone as social intruder.

Chapter 6
The Social Intruder

On an Amtrak train on its way from New York City to Washington, D.C., in 2000, I noticed the following. A couple was arguing. Not shouting at one another, no implication at all of violence, but talking loudly and heatedly enough that everyone not sound asleep five or six rows in front or behind could hear them. I looked around and noticed most of the passengers in the affected section (including me) were going about their business, ignoring the argument. Perhaps two or three people exchanged brief glances. The argument was over in a few minutes. About ten minutes later, someone else's cellphone rang, and a woman proceeded to have a conversation with a business associate. Her voice was loud, as audible as the voices of the former bickerers. As her conversation progressed, more than half the passengers in the affected area grumbled, and several complained loudly.

Why was this person who was talking long distance on the cellphone more irritating, more disruptive than the people who were arguing right in front of everyone on that train? The worst that could be said about the woman's business conversation was that it was utterly boring. I suppose a quarreling couple, in general, could have provided some interest—comic relief, cursing, whatever—but in this case the little squabble was as unremarkable as the business conversation, with no accusations of hot affairs to warrant eager attention from the people on the train. So why were they so put off by the cellphone conversation? Apparently the problem was so widespread, the cellphone conversation on trains so vexing to so many passengers, that Amtrak soon unveiled a new "amenity"

(as Amtrak likes to call its perks for passengers): a "quiet car,"
in which cellphone conversations are not allowed.

Cellphone Envy

In the early days of the cellphone—I mean in the mid-1990s,
when it first began piping up everywhere you turned—
I thought that annoyance at its use in public places stemmed
from jealousy: I'd like to have a cellphone, why don't I have
one, if I don't have a cellphone, why are those inconsiderate,
conspicuously consuming people flaunting theirs? (Thorstein
Veblen coined the term "conspicuous consumption" and first
noted the need of the wealthy and successful to proclaim their
status in his classic *Theory of the Leisure Class*, 1899/1953.)
But as the number of people with cellphones increased and the
number of annoyed people seemed to do the same, my initial
hypothesis seemed to lose some momentum.

I think it still would be interesting to take a survey of people most annoyed by others' use of cellphones—I suspect that
the most annoyed still would be those who refused cellphones
for themselves. But I also think the nature of the annoyance
may have shifted, at least a bit, from envy about not having a
cellphone, to envy about not having received a call on one's
cellphone.

There are no doubt variations on the envy emotion that
come into play here. If the person who does not receive the
cellphone call is sitting at the same table as the person who
does receive the call, or is otherwise a candidate for conversation with the person who receives the call, then the irritation
is: Why are you having a conversation with him or her rather
than with me? A classic epitome of rudeness in the cellphone
age thus has become: He or she is out on a date with me, why
is he or she talking on the phone to someone else? I first
became aware of this species of "anti-date," not from any
personal experience or even observation, but when a reporter

doing a story about cellphones for the *Washington Post* in 1999 asked me what I thought about a guy who talked on the cellphone rather than to his date as they sat in a restaurant for their first evening out. I replied either the guy's crazy, rude, both, or maybe trying to impress his date with his cellphone, which in those days was still new and cool. In my day, after all, the phone call was a conduit to an occasion, or perhaps a substitute for it, not usually an event or feature of the night on the town itself. (The story, written by Eve Zibart, was entitled "Rrring! rrring! rrring! Just when did the phone in your pocket become more irresistible than a real live person?" Other highlights of the article include cellphones ringing at a White House state dinner, a St. Alban's Christmas Eve service, a urinal at the Mongolian Grill restaurant in Bethesda, Maryland, and, of course, in the middle of all kinds of conversations in sundry establishments. I was quoted, in part, as saying cellphones are like cars: "You can drive courteously, or you can weave all over the place.")

But being snubbed as a conversation partner would not be what bothers the ubiquitous Greek chorus who look askance and cluck at cellphone use from people they do not know from Adam. For this much larger number of people, when anger at not receiving a call is not driving their attitude, we must look elsewhere for its source.

One-Sided Conversations

If eavesdropping is an art, its subject matter and reward would be the enticing, or at least worthy-of-being-overheard, conversation. The half-conversation we hear from people talking on the cellphone frustrates this noble pursuit. Hearing half a conversation may be "cool" in the McLuhanesque sense—we're invited to fill in the missing half in our mind's ear—but most people like their eavesdropped narrative a little more complete. Even television, which McLuhan thought was "cool" or incomplete in comparison to motion pictures, usually provides more than one side of a story. (In McLuhan's day, most television was small, blurry, and even black-and-white in comparison to movies on the big screen. According to McLuhan, the less information a medium provides, the "cooler" it is, the more it pulls us in. This analysis may indeed explain some of the wrathful attraction that the one-sided conversation holds for many people—drawn to it, irritated by it, embracing it, kicking and screaming, at the same time. See McLuhan's *Understanding Media*, 1964, and my *Digital McLuhan*, 1999, for more on "hot" and "cool" media.) Listening in on a one-sided conversation is thus not like listening to the radio, watching television, reading a book, or engagement with any other one-way medium that tells a more or less complete, self-contained, if not necessarily finished story. It is rather like watching a movie without sound on an airplane, because you're sitting in economy class and don't want to pay for the earphones. Except in the case of auditing someone else's conversation on the cellphone, you likely wouldn't be given the other half even if you offered payment.

Like most things cellphonic, the audience for one-sided conversations started at home, where the telephone held sway for its first century. Parental aggravation about their teenage kids talking on the phone was likely fed at least in part by the half-conversation demon, along with the more overt concerns that talking on the telephone took time away from homework, interrupted dinner with the family, and the like. But home also allowed the listener in the room certain outlets not available to the eavesdropper in public. My wife, for example, occasionally fills in pieces of my conversation—answers questions I may be asking, or comments on what I am saying—as she walks by and hears me talking on the phone. (This sometimes distracts me from the conversation I'm having, but I'm good at multitasking.) If worse comes to worst, and the annoyance of hearing someone talking on the phone at home gets too great, the aggrieved listener always can tell the person on the phone to get off already. Obviously, such techniques would be of limited value with strangers in public. Further, though it might seem to be easier to walk away from an irritating, half-overheard conversation in public than at home—there's more room to roam in public, and strangers are not likely to take offense if you slip away—often just the reverse is true. If you are in a particular place in public and have a specific reason for being there, as in a restaurant or a doctor's waiting room, you cannot easily just get up and walk away. You certainly cannot just walk off a moving bus, abuzz with the cellphones of other passengers. But absenting yourself from an annoying soliloquy at home is usually no problem, unless you share a one-room apartment.

Possibly adding to the irritation of hearing one-sided conversations in public, and the jealously of not receiving a call yourself, is something in the tone of voice of the overheard speaker. Certainly some people speak louder in cellphone than in-person conversations. I recall my grandmother, in the 1950s, speaking more loudly when she was talking to someone on the phone who lived far away, even someone in a different borough than the Bronx, where she made her home. Conversations with lucky relatives in Florida were practically shouted. Something of my grandmother's phone style seems to have rubbed off on some cellphone users. Perhaps the lack of wires, or the way the mouthpiece is tucked into the cellphone, creates an insecurity that the voice is in danger of being lost in the blue. Cellphone connections are indeed currently a lot less reliable than landlines. But speaking more loudly—stridently, sonorously, mind-numbingly yet irresistibly banally, in the ears of the eavesdroppers, like an insect bite you are drawn to and need to pick at, even though you'd rather not have been bitten in the first place—does little to help this.

So the overheard cellphone conversation has a lot not to commend itself to the world at large. But the initiating ring may be more disruptive still.

Rings of Discord

The distinguishing thing about the ring of someone else's cellphone is that, right alongside of the jealousy emotion, it can be even more annoying to someone who has a cellphone and loves it than to someone who would never touch one. This is because, at the instant of the ring, every person with a cellphone thinks the ring could be his or hers. Once the overheard party begins talking, this conditioned reflex subsides, for we at least know as an absolute fact that the call can not have been ours.

The proliferation of different, personalized rings addresses this problem only somewhat. We know, after one or two complete rings, that the call is not ours (unless we too have chosen the same snippet of Beethoven or Mozart or "Take Me Out to the Ballgame" as our ring). But at the very moment the ring begins, before we are able to discern its specific cadence, I think most people respond to the perception of just a generalized "ring!"—and, like Pavlov's dogs, we lift our heads and perk our ears, brains, and expectations. This is probably mostly unconscious, but it still takes its toll. Think about what it's like to be waiting for a table in a restaurant, and the maître d' or whoever's in charge of this announces a name that sounds a lot like yours.

I suppose that, sooner or later, as we are disappointed far more than rewarded by the cellphone ring—when the calls in crowded places so frequently turn out to be for other people, not us—we will cease to salivate, or its cellphonic equivalent. But this may take our new telepathic society a good while. The ring at home has commanded our rapt, unswerving attention for more than a century. The ring in public via bells, used in every major religion except Islam, has appealed to us for millennia. (The peals have appealed to us, hence the similarity of the words, which both derive from the same old-French *apeler*, to appeal, and the Latin *appelare*, to entreat. By the time of Middle English, *pele* meant to summon by church bell, and the religious connection was explicit.) The ring of the cellphone thus has deep roots of resonance, and is not likely to be taken lightly in either private or public places for a long time. (And as a nice coincidence, the Hebrew word for miracle— *pele*—forms the name of one Israel's cellphone carriers, Pele-Phone, as mentioned at the beginning of Chapter 1.)

That the ring in public, when the phone is someone else's, should be an annoyance is a regrettable setback for the public ring. In Europe alone, it has pealed from bells in villages, towns, and cities since at least the sixth century A.D. The tidings of church bells were not necessarily joyous, but they were always important and worthy of attention. Indeed, the pealing bell was the first instant, long-range, centralized form of mass communication. It was louder than drumming or yodeling, and went far and wide with just one bell. It was not as long range as the telegraph, but certainly more instant, and with a good thirteen centuries on Morse's creation. It predated the printing press in Europe by nearly a thousand years, and capitalized on the ear's ability to hear from any direction. (This is unlike the eye, which can see only what it looks at. McLuhan referred to this property of the ear as "acoustic space," and noted its similarity to broadcasts of electronic media, which also can be in many places at once. See my "McLuhan's Space," 1990, which also notes the similarity of acoustic space and cyberspace.) Indeed, the word "broadcast" first meant to scatter or cast seeds across wide areas. Flemish artist Johannes Stradanus captured this inherently mass appeal of acoustic media, and its revolutionary achievement by the printed press, when he captioned his engraving of a bustling sixteenth-century print shop: "Just as one voice can be heard by a multitude of ears, so single writings cover a thousand sheets." (Agassi, 1968, p. 26, has a nice picture of the engraving.)

The problem with the cellphone's ring, the source of the discord it can sow, is that, unlike the church bell, it hails from a private place, the personal pocket, but is heard in public. In contrast, the church bell begins, continues, and concludes ringing all in the public sphere. The church bell knows its place, which is everywhere, consistently public, 100 percent everybody's business, even when its peals penetrate the home. The cellphone does not know its place. Its ring can be anywhere, just for you even though I hear it, just for me even though you do not want to hear it, and this can be unsettling.

All of the disruptions of the cellphone's ring, then—all of the jealousies and irritations it engenders—can be laid at the doorstep of its being in the wrong place.

But some places are more wrong than others.

All the Wrong Places

There are three kinds of places, when it comes to the wrongness of cellphones: never wrong, always wrong, sometimes wrong.

Never wrong is the easiest to identify: It's any place you want to be when you receive or make a cellphone call, as long as no one else is within earshot. A beach, a forest, your bedroom or office with no one in it but you, a restaurant in which all other patrons have left—all of these places are never wrong as locations for a cellphone call. (Notice that I did not say the restaurant was devoid of wait staff and maître d's—you're the patron, and if no other patrons are inconvenienced, you have every right to use your cellphone as you please.) Of course, you yourself might be inconvenienced by receipt of the cellphone call, but that's another matter entirely (which we considered in the previous chapter). Here all we are talking about is when and why the ring of the cellphone and the ensuing conversation might aggravate others.

Places in which the cellphone is always wrong are almost as easy. A cellphone call can almost never be right in the midst of a funeral oration—with the exception, I suppose, of someone receiving a call from a long-lost relative of the deceased, or maybe the President of the United States, or some person whom the mourners would consider ipso facto a blessing or honor to hear from. Certain pockets of certain professionals at certain times are almost never the right places for a cellphone to ring. A surgeon in the midst of an operation would seem to be an open-and-shut case against the cellphone—unless it was conveying last-minute medical information that had life-and-death relevance to the person on the table. But, by and large, prohibited places are easy to label. (I was going to say easy to call, but that would be confusing.) The ban of cellphones in New York City theaters and museums put these locations— wrongly, I would argue—in the same place as the surgeon's operating table.

Restaurants are almost right smack dab in the middle and thus pose the greatest social dilemmas for cellphone use. High-priced restaurants seem more forbidding of cellphone conversation than coffee shops, fast-food places, and greasy spoons. I've seen signs prohibiting cellphones in even medium-priced restaurants, but never in a cafeteria or diner. Never in a McDonald's, Burger King, or Wendy's. I'm not quite sure why. The wealthy are more entitled to protection from the acoustic barrages of strangers? Likely the wealthy are just paying for the privilege of dining under the best possible conditions, or circumstances most under their control. Significantly, that includes freedom from the unwanted rings of others, at the expense of being unable to receive a call that you, a wealthy patron, may desire. It's an interesting reversal of Veblen's "conspicuous consumption": the nouveau riche start out flaunting their cellphones, but within a decade or so start dining in restaurants in which cellphone use is forbidden. Well, if you're that rich, you can no doubt hire people to take your business calls, at least, out of your earshot.

Presumably the closer the ring and conversation, the more intrusive, whatever the cuisine and cultural height of the establishment. That's why talking on the phone can be more offensive to people at your table than to people across the room, and not just because people farther away hear less of your voice. The nub of the insult comes from people at your table wanting to talk to you, or at least expecting to talk to you, in contrast to people across the room not caring if you exist, except insofar as not wanting to hear your conversation. But your dining partner also can be more considerate and tolerant of your cellphone conversation than anyone else in the restaurant, if your partner is a professional colleague or loved one or someone who for whatever reason understands how important the cellphone conversation is to you and is willing to forgo an actual or potential conversation with you in favor of whatever you are saying to the person on the phone.

The line between understanding and insult, however, can be razor thin. Is your dining partner secure enough in your relationship—business or pleasure—not to mind your talking to someone else on the phone, to even encourage it? It all depends on the nature of your relationship to the person in front of you, as well as your relationship to the person on the phone, and the differences can be as subtle and profound as a heartbeat.

This point about relationships in place prior to the receipt or placement of the cellphone call is in many ways the most crucial, because it suggests that underlying all of the factors that determine if a cellphone conversation is offensive to an audience is this basic question: What is the emotional or other connection of the spectator to the talker? Such psychological connections govern the impact of the overheard cellphone connection. If the audience has no emotional or other expectation of you, then the worst that can result from witnessing your cellphone conversation is annoyance. Any prior investment in you or your time raises the stakes.

Indeed, nothing about the cellphone and its impact can be understood without recourse to relationships—between caller and receiver, audience and speaker, and even among just the members of the audience themselves. A group of friends, devoted to their own conversation, are less likely to be annoyed by someone outside of their group speaking on the cellphone than would a group of unrelated individuals, with time on their hands and attention to burn.

The cellphone is so intrinsically a social instrument that considering its impact on the individual, outside of a relationship to others, physically present or not, is bound to be inadequate. You cannot, after all, talk to yourself on the phone, as you can browse alone for information on the Web, or watch television, or listen to the radio, or read a book on your own. (It is actually quite difficult to read a book *not* on your own, unless you have someone else read it to you entirely, in which case you really are listening to the book, not reading it. Reading is also, as discussed in Chapter 3, quite possessive. You can get most of what a radio is saying or singing to you with someone else in the room talking to you. Certainly you can do this with television. But paying attention to anything else when you are reading means you have stopped reading.)

In the next chapter we consider the impact of the cellphone on the most fundamental of human relationships—the family—from the romantic relationships that engender it, to parent–child relationships that ensue.

Chapter 7
Kids on the Hook

If there ever was a true technological fable about a device long sought after which, once possessed, had quite the reverse of the benefit expected, it would be the strange tale of the telephone and the teenager.

It would begin in the 1950s, when the telephone was some seventy-five years into its existence. But it wasn't until the 1950s that most Americans had phones in their homes and teenagers were in a position to use them. This was a breakout time for more than one technology that would change society. Televisions were being installed even faster than telephones in homes. Cities were spilling into suburbs, traversable mainly by automobiles.

All of these sleek new technologies became bones of contention in the family. Who would drive the automobile? A teenager who drove away in a car was beyond parental supervision. Who would determine what was watched on television? Long before the "remote" and endless fights over who controls it, my sister and I—children, not teenagers, in the 1950s—had chronic arguments over what would be watched on TV. My father, I recall, was still happy at the prospect of watching just about anything on this big magic box, so my mother adjudicated.

But disputes over the telephone were on another level entirely, for the telephone clashed, it is not too much to say, with the very sanctity of the family. Parental authority was challenged and undermined by the phone call, both made and received. Teenagers correctly saw the phone as a lifeline to the most important things in their lives—conversations with their friends, boyfriends, girlfriends. Given the choice of meat loaf and peas—or even steak—or a phone call from a friend during dinnertime, what kid would opt for the plate? As phones and soon separate phone lines began showing up in everyone's bedroom—I had one when I was sixteen, in 1963 (I did pay for it with money I earned at Krum's, a soda fountain place on the Grand Concourse in the Bronx)—the classic punishment of "go to your room," where you were supposed to commune with your conscience, became worthless. (The installation of televisions and eventually computers in kids' rooms had a similar, undermining effect. Banishment to your room became exile in the infinite world of people and information beyond it, in most cases far more interesting than the people and information in your immediate surroundings outside the room.)

In all of these tussles over the telephone, the teenager was striving to have one, or at least have access to one, and the parent was resisting.

No one could have predicted that the day would soon come when parents would insist that their kids each have a phone, and turned on at all times.

The Gripping Hand

Children have been a special concern of media critics since at least the beginning of the twentieth century. Back then, observers worried about the adverse effect of movies on kids— in William A. McKeever's "Motion Pictures: A Primary School for Criminals" in the 1910 *Good Housekeeping* magazine, for example, the professor from Kansas argues that dank movie theaters where kids wile away their afternoons are destroying the moral backbone of our future. By the middle of the century, the locus of presumed peril had shifted to comic books and television. Marie Wynn's *The Plug-In Drug* (1977) may be the best known of the many attacks against TV. She contends that watching it can be addictive, especially for children. In a society in which even love has been said to be addictive, I guess this isn't too much of a metaphorical stretch. But the points of actual similarity between real, physical addictions such as heroin and psychological "addictions" such as television are nil. (Jerry Mander went even further in his 1978 book, *Four Arguments for the Elimination of Television*, seriously suggesting that watching television might cause cancer.)

By the end of the twentieth century, the villain was the Internet. Hence the Communications Decency Act of 1996, wisely struck down as unconstitutional by the Supreme Court, provided for fines of up to $100,000 and two years' imprisonment for the publishing of "indecent" material on the Web, if the material was in any manner accessible by children. (See my *The Soft Edge*, 1997, and "The Cellphone at War" in Chapter 10 of the current book for more.) Thus the Internet has made television look respectable in comparison, in the same way as television earlier helped lift motion pictures somewhere closer to the status of the "legitimate" theater (itself bawdy in Shakespeare's time). It is certainly true that children cannot be stalked via television, and, for that reason alone, parents are justified in feeling more comfortable with their kids being couch potatoes than Web riders. (On the subject of children and the Internet, incidentally, there is a world of difference between pornographic Web pages that may be accessible by people under the legal age of adulthood and sexual predators using the Internet to stalk people of any age. The first is a question of freedom of expression, right to access information, whether society has the right to legally define obscenity, and so on. The second is simply a vicious crime, online and off-line. On countering that crime, the Web can be an important weapon for distributing information to the public about known sexual predators, including what they look like and their whereabouts.)

How does the cellphone figure in this historic, ongoing dilemma about children and media? As a fundamentally interactive, two-way interpersonal instrument, the cellphone is very different from the above cases. Motion pictures, television, and pornography on the Web provide non-interactive, one-way information. Predators on the Web are obviously interactive, or trying to be, but unlike the cellphone, the Web easily provides contact to strangers, which is one of its dangers for children.

Do we have any cause to be concerned about the adverse impact of cellphones on kids? I would say yes—but not because it exposes them to material objected to by parents. Rather, we perhaps need to be concerned because the cellphone makes kids too accountable to parents.

There was a time—indeed, throughout all of human history—when teenagers could be away from their parents. This seems like a simple, obvious fact of life. You want to get away from your parent, you just walk out of the house. But the cellphone makes that kind of everyday getaway impossible, absent the provocation of the teenager shutting the phone off or lying about its lack of service.

Of course, up to a certain age, children should not be long out of touch with their parents, or at least a responsible adult. But teenagers are a different story. Biologically adult, yet legally and socially "minor," the teenager often must endure adult urges without the wherewithal to act on them. The telephone in the home allowed the teenager to act like an adult, at least insofar as information was concerned. The telephone doesn't ask your age, doesn't require a card to use—well, not the kind of card or proof of age required for admission to R-rated movies. You were under your parents' roof and supervision at home, all right, but if you were on the phone, you were miles beyond them.

Why not extend this ability to times you were outside the home? Pay phones did (and still do) this, but the cellphone does it much better. You can call anyone, at any time, from anywhere you like, and anyone can similarly call you. But . . .

That "anyone" can include your parents, the very adults whose scrutiny you wanted to escape in the first place. And the cellphone makes it easy not only for your parents to call you, but for you to call them. In some ways that's worse, because it puts the onus on you. The phone in your pocket pickpockets your excuses not to call home at a given time. And if for some good reason you do not, your parents always have the recourse of calling you.

The cellphone thus extends and strengthens the sinews of family. For better or worse—and the effects are likely both—there is no place anyone can be away from family now. Whereas previously the family shared both physical space and communication in the home, and to leave the home was to leave both the physical space and most of the communication, nowadays the cellphone keeps the family's communication intact when the home is left behind. From the point of view of family communication, the physical home becomes less relevant, less essential. Instead, the mobile hearth provides some of the crucial family functions. The cellphone is thus a mobile hearth not only because it provides access to so many different kinds of information, but because the core of that information is familial. Important aspects of family become retrievable, implementable, anywhere, by the mere press of a thumb.

Why would this in any way be detrimental? Isn't family, in general, good, and its strengthening therefore desirable? Yes. But part of growing up, part of becoming an adult, and therefore part of the proper function of family, is also leaving the family. Not entirely. Not even necessarily physically. But certainly this means moving from a state in which parents should and do keep tabs on just about every activity of their children to a state in which they do not. Indeed, we might define the passage of childhood into adulthood as a transformation of parent/children tabs from mandatory to voluntary.

Joshua Meyrowitz, in his *No Sense of Place* (1985), suggested that equal access of parents and children to information on television—information previously available only to fully literate adults, for example, news reported in newspaper stories, now on television—was making children much more like adults. Certainly the coverage of the terrorist attacks on September 11, 2001, and the Iraqi War in 2003 on 24/7 all-news cable stations gave children complete access to the information their parents were receiving about these events. Children using the Web also are often in the same informational realms as adults (hence the concern about exposure of children to pornography—not a reason to censor the Web, for reasons I explained above, but nonetheless worthy of note by parents). But cellphones, which at first seem to continue this trend by giving children who have them the same access as their parents to the world of people with phones, may ironically cut against this trend in the end. In keeping children and teenagers more accountable to their parents, the cellphone safeguards the distinction between child and adult—the distinction between the accountable one (the teenager) and the one who must be accounted to (the parent). But if the cellphone does this too long and too well—if it keeps the teenager too long on the apron string, on the towline cell line of omni-accountability—then the cellphone could become a leash that impedes the growth of child to independent adult.

The cellphone is actually an excellent assistant on both sides of this transformational process—the little child before and the complete adult after—just not in the middle, at the point of transformation, the teenage turning point. The cellphone works well for parents who must keep in touch with children and children who must keep in touch with their parents, and it also works well for adult children who want, who elect, to be in touch with *their* parents. But the cellphone and its 24/7 accessibility can work at cross-purposes with the transitional stage where children are just becoming adults, are taking the first full steps toward informational self-sufficiency, or unaccountability to parents.

The cellphone has not been around long enough for us to gauge this potentially stultifying effect on teenagers. But if the effect is real, its remedy will reside in appropriate social attitudes that limit cellphonic access to teenagers. (Note, again, that what would need restriction here is not access of teenagers to the world at large but access *to* teenagers by parents.) As with other possible social disruptions of the cellphone, the solution, again, would be in more sharply defined custom.

Husbands and Wives on Call

Parents and children are not the only components of family whose relationships are being altered, even revolutionized, by the cellphone. Husbands and wives now enjoy the same ubiquity of access—not only to the world, but to one another.

The access between husbands and wives, unlike that of parents and children, is supposed to be discretionary, at least in principle—either partner is perfectly within his or her rights to choose not to make or receive a call. And, in practice prior to the cellphone, it usually was, certainly for husbands and wives who were not at home. (Anyone at home was and still is by and large expected to answer the phone, if not physically indisposed.) But, as we have already seen with the cellphone and its impact, the mere possibility or option of being in phone contact, where previously there was none or the contact was difficult to attain, subtly yet fundamentally changes the chemistry of expectations.

Until recently there was an intrinsic buffer between family life and business, between the wife who was at home and the husband who was at work, between the husband who was at home and the wife who was at work, between husband and wife in both directions when both were at work. The only easy call to make was from the person at work to the person at home. The other way around was not so easy. The workplace was effectively shielded from the home—not impenetrably, but layered, like a coat with many linings. Long ago, in order to reach a white-collar person at work, the caller had to go through the white collar's secretary. Blue-collar workers were even more removed from phones; their bosses, if they chose, could interrupt their work with word of someone on the phone for them in the office (assuming the workers were anywhere near the office, which they very well might not be). Directly dialable phone numbers and extensions eliminated the intermediaries in many places, but the white collar anyplace away from the desk was still unreachable, or not easily reachable, during the business day. The cellphone has altered every bit of that, stripped all the layers away. It rings right in the pocket of white- or blue-collar workers, regardless of what kinds of jackets with how many linings they may wear.

The home had already been under siege from office work for nearly a decade, courtesy of e-mail and the Internet, which allows people to conduct business from the bedroom or anyplace in the home with a computer and a modem or other means of data transmission. We could say the Internet made the bedroom a suitable place for intercourse in the older, once-primary use of the term—communication and transactions, for commerce and friendship, among sundry people, including strangers. The cellphone injects this homogenization of business and personal life right back into the office. The result is a world with fewer and fewer places where just business or just pleasure can be pursued. (And in this realm—the business/pleasure continuum—the cellphone thus does what Meyrowitz says television does for adults and children: It blurs distinctions.)

There are numerous practical advantages to this always being in touch. I much prefer getting a call from someone in my family telling me we need juice or milk or cookies, as I walk from my office to my car or as I'm driving home, than finding out about it after I have passed all the supermarkets and convenience stores, parked my car in the driveway, and walked through my front door. The undeniable benefit of the cellphone is that it sooner or later provides us with useful information that we would not otherwise possess. Coming from a past of information scarcity and cloistering—in which to drive or be driven in a car meant that we were out of touch with everyone not in the car—we are undeniably in the market for the helpful, timely phone call. Still, one might say to the cellphone enthusiast: Be patient, you'll get the information sooner or later anyway, life wasn't so unbearable twenty years ago, was it? No, it was not. But that's no reason why we should have to wait now, be inconvenienced, when the cellphone is at hand.

But neither should we be blind to the way that the cellphone and its revolution in access can refigure the very relationship it benefits. Was there ever a time in history when husbands and wives, parents and children, families, were in such close continuing contact? The family on the farm often has been cited as the predecessor to the digital homestead. But unless husband and wife and children worked literally together in the field all day, even the farmstead lacked the unrelieved continuity of contact of the "cellstead." Any time Farmer Jones was out with the crops and the Missus was home cooking up a stew, this husband and wife had more communicative space between them than today's enlightened couples with cellphones.

Is a certain amount of informational distance necessary for a good marriage? Hard to say. Divorce rates certainly were high prior to cellphones. Cellphones probably make infidelity more difficult. Well, they certainly make being plausibly out of touch with a spouse more difficult, but they also can facilitate communication between the parties of indiscretions, so maybe it's a draw. Cellphones certainly make henpecking and its male equivalent easier. But they also allow faster apologies—that is, apologies made more shortly after whatever the offense—and that's probably good. I recall wanting to apologize to my girlfriend for something I had said, as I watched her take off in a plane to London way back in the early 1970s. I was reduced to sending a telegram to her hotel: "Hi Honey, I'm sorry. . . . Here's a big kiss. . . ." I had to spell out each word on the phone to the disinterested voice in the Western Union telegraph office. "Right, that's 'kiss,' k,i,s,s. . . ." The cellphone offers a refreshing antithesis to this painful, comical, circuitous route of the telegram. (Conveying the content of my telegram by telephone made things even worse, in this case. Had I written out my message and hand-delivered it to the guy in the telegraph office, at least I would not have had to spell out "k-i-s-s" to him. But it worked out okay in the long run—my girlfriend, Tina, became my wife, and we've been happily married for more than a quarter century.)

The cellphone thus can make it easier to say something nice. And not only apologies. A cellphone can speed and facilitate the communication of good news, good feelings, anything that we don't want to wait to get home to convey. . . . But impulse cellphoning also speeds expression of pique, which is probably not so good. If the same device quickens soothing and venting— "Honey, I'm sorry I was such an idiot before," and "Honey, you know I was thinking about what you said, and I'm really furious"—then the net effect on this aspect of marriage may end up a wash, after all.

Whatever the impact of the cellphone on squabbling, it certainly serves to equalize the roles of husbands and wives in families. We already have moved in the past fifty years to fathers who spend more time with their children and mothers who spend more time earning money. By making connections to business and family equally easy, the cellphone is further transforming fathers and mothers into uniform, interchangable, all-purpose parents who have the same relationship to their children, providing the same mixture of nurturing and distance, the same combination of emotional and economic support.

There was a time, not very long ago, when differences between men and women, including husbands and wives, were celebrated. Critics of that age have pointed out, correctly, that "vive la différence!" masked injustices, unfair restrictions of behavior, mostly for women. One of the challenges of the cellphone age will be to make sure that such differences as are worth celebrating, that men and women may choose (not be required) to pursue, remain available.

We next examine the impact of the cellphone on the very nucleus of vive la différence, at the very origin of family: romance.

Romancing the Phone

As *Bye Bye Birdie* (the 1963 movie from a 1959 Broadway play) portrayed so well, the telephone has been an indispensable agent of romance for at least half a century. Flirting, asking someone out, giggling about crushes, boasting about conquests, confessing true love, breaking up—all have been amply served by the faceless acoustic intimacy of the telephone. Indeed, the phone is itself a highly sensual instrument. When you speak on the phone, your lips graze the mouthpiece, your voice travels to an earpiece far away, against which is tightly pressed the ear of the person who hears you. The effective psychological distance between the two of you is intimate. You're talking right into her or his ear. Your lips—and breath—seem a hairsbreadth away. Only lovers or very close friends or members of the family enjoy such proximity off the phone. Although sexually explicit talk is just one of many possible kinds of conversation on the phone, it is not at all surprising that it occurs, along with more general romantic exchanges and chatter.

Phones were apparently that way from the beginning. Fifty years before *Bye Bye Birdie*, Valentine's Day and other postcards from the early decades of the twentieth century were filled with pictures of people on phones, and captions flirtatious and sexually suggestive. "Sweetheart Send Me A Kiss By Wire," a leather postcard copyright by W. S. Neal inveighs. That was one of the sweeter ones, with the "heart" in the shape of a Valentine, and the words "kiss" and "wire" written in script that smoothes into wires at either end, which connect into phones employed by a gent and a lady, lips and ears by the mouthpiece and earpiece. "Now You Are Getting Too

Personal," another postcard, sent December 4, 1910, advises, with a picture of an embarrassed but delighted young woman seated and talking, rolling her eyes, on the phone. Apropos the discussion of witnesses to phone conversations in the previous chapter, one of my favorite cards, dated July 31, 1905 (copyright that year by the U. S. Souvenir Postcard Company), is entitled "What Tales the Telephone Girl Could Tell," and shows a telephone operator listening in on a conversation between two rather happy gentlemen. "Hot stuff, eh Bill?" "Great shape." "A regular peach." "What did your wife say?" are among the tidbits she overhears. Presumably the telephone operator at the turn of the last century was a less aggravated eavesdropper—at least, for these sorts of conversations—than the general public for cellphone conversations today.

By the 1940s, the postcards became more explicit. A "Mutoscope Card" with a hot red background depicts a Betty Grable type, clad only in high heels and a transparent negligee, seated, legs crossed, by her phone (by now a "French" phone, with earpiece and mouthpiece in one unit), but not in use. "There Must Be Something Wrong With My Line," her caption informs us. (Certainly there is nothing wrong with her leg lines.) And speaking of lines, a card from a few years earlier has little hearts running across the wires, connected to a telephone inside a big heart, and says, "By Telephone or Wireless, Whatever be the line, Just tell me that you love me, and I'm Your Valentine." (See Figures 7.1, 7.2, 7.3, 7.4, and 7.5.)

If love is blind, it surely met one of its two ideal media in phone lines. (The other would be love letters—written lines.) The last caption, however, is especially interesting, since it mentions not only the telephone, but the newer "wireless," which, in those days (approximately 1910 to 1920) would have meant a call via radio. That would have been far more expensive and unlikely than a phone call, which perhaps would have made such a radio call an even greater demonstration of love. How will love play out on today's inexpensive, omnipresent wireless cellphone?

Figure 7.1. "Sweetheart Send Me A Kiss By Wire"

As always, what the cellphone most changes is accessibility—giving both parties to the romance much more of it—to each other, and to everyone around them. How many romances might have been, but never were, because no one was at home when the phone was ringing? Telephone answering machines—voice mail, in today's parlance—can remedy this, but only sometimes. People routinely place calls, get voice mail, and elect to leave no message, for matters far less emotionally precarious than asking someone out on a date. In the service of true love, the almost always available cellphone thus can be truly heroic.

At the same time, a delay in accessibility sometimes can help, as with so much else in human affairs. I remember on more than one occasion calling a girl for the first time, being fairly nervous, and receiving just an endless ring. When I called back an hour later, I was considerably more relaxed (and, I believed, more cool). Who knows what damage I would have done to my chances had I gotten through the first time?

But there also may be something less romantic in talking on the run, or anyplace on the move—this relates, again, to the

Figure 7.2. "Now You are Getting Too Personal"

question of place and phone. Cuddling up in a comfortable chair seems a better place to talk about boyfriends, girlfriends, sex, and love than a crowded street or a bus. (I heard a professor at New York University talk in the late 1970s about an informal study she had conducted with her teenaged daughter. She had videotaped her telephone conversations and noted that her postures—the way she stretched out in bed, lounged in a chair, moved her arms and legs around her while talking on the phone—were sexual. The conversations were presumably with girlfriends, about boys.) On the other hand, a quiet

Figure 7.3. "What Tales the Telephone Girl Could Tell"

beach or a clearing near a lake could be an even better setting for a romantic conversation.

The same presumably would apply to phone sex. Indeed, even more so. (At the very least, phone sex on a crowded train, or anywhere in viewable public, would likely not be tolerated, certainly not by police, if it entailed any kind of obvious masturbation by the person in view.) There is no record that I know of detailing when the first phone sex happened—when "I love you" and "I want you" changed to "I'm slowly unbuttoning your clothes. . . ." If the telephone postcards and their innuendos are any indication, phone sex probably goes back as far as romance on the phone. By the 1980s, the first publicly commercial phone-sex services were in operation. Customers called numbers advertised in magazines and paid with credit cards. Receipts exceeded $4 billion by 1999. (According to "Pornography Statistics" published by Family Safe Media, they reached $4.5 billion worldwide in 2003.)

Although cellphones might not be ideal instruments for phone sex in public, they certainly open up possibilities in the out-of-the-way places, indoor and outdoor, unreachable by phone lines. And the advent of Internet cellphone connections

Figure 7.4. "There Must be Something Wrong With My Line"

and Palm Pilots has provided a pictorial accompaniment, phone sex on a tableau of porn. Even the tactile dimension has come into play: In 2003, Vibelet's "Purry Kitty" software was unveiled. It turns certain Nokia cellphones into vibrators. One could say this marks the reversal of the two-way cellphone into a one-way medium. (McLuhan had noted that when media play out their potential, they "flip" or "reverse" into a different use, often bearing characteristics of much earlier media. See his "Laws of the Media," 1977, and my *Digital McLuhan*, 1999, Chapter 15, "Spirals of Media Evolution."

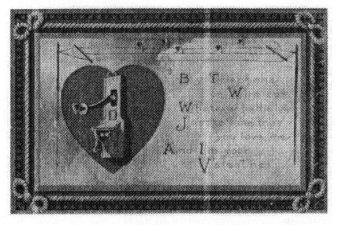

Figure 7.5. "By Telephone or Wireless . . ."

McLuhan also predicted that the next step after the audiovisual "massage" of television was the tactile.) The Purry Kitty
certainly lends support to the updated Mae West quip about
cigars and pockets: "Is that a cellphone in your pocket, or are
you just happy to see me?"

But aside from ringing phones as vibrators, the main impact
of the cellphone, like the telephone before it, has been on two-
way relationships, romantic and sexual, faithful and otherwise. At very least, if you're cheating on your girlfriend or
boyfriend, the cellphone makes you more vulnerable to discovery. Whether this will have the effect of making couples
more faithful or making cheating more acceptable is unclear,
just as it is for husbands and wives. The ethics of the ever-
reachable, telepathic society are not yet settled, because the
society is still very much under construction.

One bemoaned consequence of the telephone, however,
even before cellphones, was that it seemed to herald the end of
the great art of love letters. After all, why trust your passions
to the slow post, when you can pick up a phone and convey
them immediately? The telephone postcards already described
are thus a revealing transitional medium, in which one writes

to one's love or love interest, "Why don't you call me?" Indeed, many telephone postcards said just that, either in a printed caption that came with the card or written in specifically in the sender's scribbled message. A card from 1910 sent to someone in Dallas, Texas, has it all: "Will you" is written in by the sender, above the caption "Call To-morrow." But the full personal message, on the other side of the card, has a twist—it's from one guy to another, who inquires of his friend, "Did you go *dear* hunting? *Ha, ha.*" (See Figure 7.6.)

In effect, the postcard petitioners were using a slow, relatively permanent medium (the pen on paper in the mail) to request a fast, live, fleeting response (the phone call). A "Banforth Company" postcard from around 1920 took a slightly different tack on the same mixed media environment and offered a little primer that warms the heart of a media historian: "Some folk write in Pencil" (picture of a pencil), "Some folk write in Ink" (quill in inkwell), "Some folk send a Telegram" (telegraph pole with wires), "Some type in a wink" (typewriter), "Some folk use telephone" (two-piece telephone), "Some send a wireless call" (radio with phonograph-ear speaker), "But some of course use none of these, Or ever write at all!" And on the side of the card, the title "Why Not Write" appears—in other words, an inducement to at least scrawl something and send back a postcard, if you're unlikely to use any other kind of more modern communication. The logic makes sense. In fact, it appeals to the possible sender of the postcard, before it is purchased, inscribed, and mailed. After all, this very postcard would have been right in the hand of anyone reading it. How much effort would it have taken to buy it, write a sweet note, affix a penny stamp, and put it in the mailbox? But, alas, in the case of this postcard in my possession, the persuasion was mostly unavailing. Perhaps it was purchased. But the postcard is as pure as the driven snow, touched by neither pencil nor pen. (Well, we can still be optimistic: Maybe the guy read it, put it back on the shelf of the general store, and ran home and called.) (See Figure 7.7.)

(a)

(b)

Figure 7.6(a) and (b). "Call To-morrow" (both sides)

Figure 7.7. "Some folk write in Pencil. . . ."

In any event, written exhortations to call, if they worked, had the effect of shifting communication from writing to speaking. It would take the advent of e-mail in the 1980s to retrieve the written word, and this indeed was the first progress in electronic text since the telegraph. The triumph of text on personal computers was predictable—certainly in retrospect—since computers use screens. Much less expected was the cellphone as an upstart champion of letters.

In the next chapter we consider the cellphone as a vehicle of communication other than spoken conversation.

Chapter 8

More than a Conversation Piece: Texting, Texting, 1, 2, 3...

I remember the first time I received a text message on my cellphone. I had been signing one of my science fiction novels at a bookstore in downtown Philadelphia and I was walking to the 30th Street train station with a friend. My cellphone beeped quietly—only I could hear it. I took it out of my pocket, saw that a text message was waiting, and displayed it on the tiny screen. (My wife was relaying some important news—she had just gotten off the phone with one of my colleagues from my university.)

That was in 1999. What struck me about the value of receiving a communication in this way was that it was not the least bit intrusive—I was no ruder to my friend than if I had just pulled a piece of paper out of my pocket and glanced at it. My wife had sent me a text rather than a voice message for two reasons: First, there was no way, at least then, to deliberately send a voice message without a live ring. So, her choice was between (a) calling me on the cellphone and leaving a voice message if I didn't respond, or (b) sending a text message. But since my wife wasn't sure if I had finished my signing at the bookstore and didn't want to interrupt me there with a phone call, she sent the text message. Second, she wanted to convey very specific, precise information, including the phone number of my colleague in New York. A text message seemed a more reliable way to convey this.

These advantages of text were not surprising. Writing always has been more quiet than speaking (except, perhaps, in the early days, when it was chiseled with sharp stones into walls), and more precise. What was surprising was finding the written word in an instrument intended for spoken conversation, the cellphone.

But by 1999 the cellphone was well on its way to becoming a mobile hearth, as we discussed in Chapter 4—a home away from home, a home on the go, with a full panoply of communication possibilities and outlets like those found in the home. If the Internet is the medium of media, the cellphone has done one better than the Internet and is becoming the medium of media on the move. Here we take a look at how several of these lettered modes of communication play out on the phone.

The Renaissance of Text

Back in the bad old days of just old media, many pundits saw a mortal conflict between electronics and print—between watching television, listening to radio, going to the movies, on the one hand, and reading books, newspapers, and magazines, on the other. Admittedly, movies were not exactly electronic in those days—they were photochemical and mechanical—but they were seen as having the same distracting effect as television and radio on literacy. For that matter, so was the phonograph and its music, which until the 1950s was also mechanical, as in wind-up Victrolas, not electronic.

Indeed, the same complaints about motion pictures at the beginning of the twentieth century were lodged against television fifty years later: too easy an alternative to reading, too visually enthralling. Professor McKeever's complaint in 1910 that motion pictures "impart their lessons directly through the senses" (in his article "The Moving Picture: A Primary School for Criminals," discussed in Chapter 7) echoed through many decades and diatribes and eventually found its way into claims such as Marie Wynn's that television was a "plug-in drug" and Neil Postman's that watching TV was destructive not only of literacy but civility, and perhaps even civilization. (Interestingly, the first serious exploration of motion pictures as a wonderful tableau for the study of human perception and cognition was published just six years later, in 1916, by another professor—Hugo Münsterberg of Harvard University. His *Photoplay: A Psychological Study* was generally neglected by media theorists and critics until its reprinting by Dover in 1970.)

The charges against pictorial and acoustic media were plain and simply wrong from the very beginning. Motion pictures from *Gone With the Wind* through *The Godfather* have sparked reciprocal relationships with their novels, in which screen and page each benefited from the other's public attention. And the mutually supportive process continues: my 16-year-old daughter in 2002 eagerly devoured the whole of Tolkien's *Lord of the Rings* after seeing the first movie in Peter Jackson's films of the trilogy. As for television, a careful statistical comparison of reading scores in Indiana in 1944, on the eve of TV, and in 1978, found no decline whatsoever. (See Gene Maeroff, "Reading Achievement in Indiana Found as Good as in '44," 1978.) But probably the most decisive refutation of the decades of hand-wringing about television and literacy and children, and a century of the same about motion pictures, came in the hundreds of millions of copies of J. K. Rowling's *Harry Potter* novels that have sold in the past few years. In June 2003 alone, more than eight million copies of the fifth novel in the series—*Harry Potter and the Order of the Phoenix*—were shipped in the United States. For those who did not recognize the continuing life and vibrancy of the written word before, Rowling's novel was aptly named.

E-mail and personal computing, for their part, have provided for nearly a quarter of a century a continuing and growing example of an electronic medium in the service of literacy. And if this didn't convince some critics—Postman saw computers polluting as much as did television the better things in intellectual life (see his *Technopoly: The Surrender of our Culture to Technology*, 1992), and Sven Birkerts called for *Gutenberg Elegies*, mourning *The Fate of Reading in an Electronic Age* in 1994—parents certainly had no problem recognizing that computers helped rather than hindered their children's homework.

Indeed, in the 1980s, prior to the visually appealing Web, the personal computer was first and foremost a word machine—a "word processor," as it often was called then, that also did other things. (Personal computers dedicated completely to writing and printing were called word processors. Computers that telecommunicated, "managed" data, and so forth in addition to writing were said to have word-processing capabilities.) The personal computer was, after all, outfitted with a keyboard, just like the typewriter. The advent of the Web in the 1990s diluted the written word, at least somewhat, by adding icons, pictures, pointing and clicking, and sounds to the online mix. Even so, it's fair to say that the Internet still runs on written words. Not only e-mail, but online shopping, searching for information, and of course instant messaging is conducted via fingers on the keyboard.

Fingers also have triggered conversation on telephones and cellphones, from rotary dials to keypads. But the rise of text messaging on the phone is more surprising than the success of writing on the Web. Even in the days of card-punching mainframes, computers were instructed by written words. Programming is a kind of written language. But why write on the phone, when you can just as easily speak? Why text, when you can talk?

Presumably writing was invented in the first place, way back when, because there was no way to record speech or send it beyond the boundaries of earshot. Indeed, there would not be until the invention of telephone and phonograph in the 1870s. I have often thought that were a time traveler with a bag of tiny tape recorders, and a bigger supply of tiny batteries, to go back to the caves of Lascaux—or the mountain passes of the Paleolithic Alps, or the riverbanks of Pleistocene China, or anyplace else where writing might have originated with records that survived or perished—and if this time traveler had befriended some of the human inhabitants and taught them how to use the tape recorders, then writing might never have caught on or even been invented at all. At least not in those places.

But in the absence of such an impossible angel, writing came into the breach and served as a fine second best. Cave art evolved into hieroglyphics, eventually supplanted, in most parts of the world, by alphabetic writing, which was greatly augmented, some three millennia later, by the printing press in the West, and four centuries after that by the telegraph. This last was an impressive invention indeed. It conveyed words across long distances at the speed of electricity or light, which was tantamount to the speed of speech at short range. But the words were written.

Thus the appeal of the telephone and its spoken conversation was obvious and irresistible. It eventually swept away the telegraph and its long-distance text messaging. Not until e-mail and fax in the 1980s would text re-enter the mainstream of instant, global communication.

But the battle between text on the telegraph and voices on the phone was not just a clear-cut contest of writing versus speaking. The phone also had an inside advantage: it conveyed voices directly into homes and places of business. No third party, no person in a smart uniform, had to knock on your door and deliver a telephone message. Pneumatic tubes, as we saw in Chapter 4, helped the telegraph at least a little in that area, by whisking telegrams right into business offices. But the telephone still had the upper hand, the better hand, because no hands of strangers ever touched its messages, even for a minute. With the phone, no words of love or sensitive business had to be entrusted to a stranger or anyone not party to the conversation—as had been the case and would continue to be with street mail and telegrams, regardless of how rapidly they were delivered. No, the words of the telephone came, really special delivery, right into the ear of the recipient.

Text on the cellphone now at last competes on an equal footing: text and voice alike are instantly, immediately, directly delivered to you and only you as you walk down the street, sit on a hill, recline on a blanket at the beach (and, to the chagrin of some teachers, if you're sitting in a classroom, too). In this new, cellphonic context, the silence, precision, and endurance of text—the advantages it always had over voice—finally are able to show their mettle.

What a difference a century made: A hundred years ago motion pictures and radio were about to vie with books, and telephone calls outnumbered telegrams ten to one. Today text rules the Internet and in some parts of the world accounts more than spoken conversation for cellphone use. Moreover, text on the phone seems to be making its greatest inroads among younger users. A variety of surveys in 2002 and 2003 reported that 35 percent of young adults used their cellphones for texting, in contrast to 20 percent of all users. Fifty percent of eighteen to twenty-four-year-old cellphone users claimed to be interested in sending and receiving text messages, in comparison to 35 percent of all users. Worldwide, estimates are that text messaging and its refinements will account for 85 percent of "youth spending" on their cellphones by 2006, with ring tones in second place. (Data reported by Telephia, Harris Interactive, and Wireless World Forum; see Robyn Greenspan, "Look Who's Talking, Texting, Buying," 2003, for more details.) Thus the very kids whose literacy was thought by McKeever, Postman, Wynn, and many others for almost a hundred years to be jeopardized by electronic media are now leading the triumph of text on the cellphone. Dan Wilton named them "Generation Text." (This written revolution includes instant messaging on personal computers, as well; see Dunnewind, 2003, for details.)

Critics already have objected that the truncated text on cellphone (and computer) screens is hardly great literature, to read or write. (For a worse than usual tantrum, see Jenn Young's "i h8 imspk," 2003.) But neither were most Victorian letters, or postcards with a few scribbled lines, or staccato telegrams dashed off well before the advent of television. The essential point about texting is that it is written, meaning that its creation and comprehension derives from a part of our mentality different from what we use to hear or see images. Whether the agent of composition is the traditional index finger and thumb holding a pen or pencil, or index and middle finger pecking away on a keyboard, or the now-cool, au courant thumb on the cellphone (the small phone is cradled in one hand, freeing the other hand for other tasks, leaving the conveniently opposable thumb on the first hand ready for texting use), makes no difference. Neither does whether the words are received on paper, big computer screen, or the little screen of the cellphone. Nor does the pace, style, or particular mix of symbolic tools of the writing.

There is nothing inherently inferior about "h8" as an abbreviation for "hate." Indeed, "h8" uses an ancient rebus method—you write the word "belief" by drawing pictographs of a bee and a leaf, which when spoken yield "belief"—that was one of the most creative aspects of Egyptian hieroglyphics. If somehow texting led to a complete loss of the alphabet and a return to the prehistoric reliance on pictures for writing, that might be a cause for concern. But, in fact, short messaging on cellphones and computer screens represents a resurgence of the alphabet over the Mac and Windows icon. The words in instant and short messaging may be spiced with an icon or two—just as traditional text employs italics and exclamation points—but they are alphabetic, through and through. Their readers and writers are as literate as you and I. Indeed, maybe more so, in my case, since texters are creating a slightly new form of writing from various components, whereas I am doing the best I can, here, with an already existing form.

Not only are cellphone texters retrieving older writing techniques like the rebus, but they are doing this with the unlikely appendage of their thumbs. Charles Darwin noted way back in 1862, in *On the Various Contrivances by Which British and Foreign Orchids Are Fertilised by Insects*—published just three years after his *The Origin of Species*, which brought his theory of natural selection to the world—how organic characteristics and structures, naturally selected and adapted to do a specific kind of task in an environment, also can work beautifully doing different sorts of things in new environments that were not in existence when the organism first evolved. Evolutionary biologists from George Gaylord Simpson to Stephen Jay Gould have identified this kind of "preadaptation"—a body part serving well in a task that had nothing to do with its initial evolution—as one of the key mechanisms of life on Earth. (See my *Mind at Large: Knowing in the Technological Age*, 1988, Chapter 3, for more.) Use of mammalian walking limbs for bat wings and seal swimming paddles are prime examples. And now, several hundred thousand or more years into the human technological information age, so is our thumb on the cellphone. The opposable thumb first enabled our emergence as an upright, bipedal, intelligent species, by enabling us to grasp objects and tools. Indeed, some of those may well have been early instruments of writing, or at least marking. Today the thumb turns out to work admirably in a brand-new, unexpected task, the grasping and launching of written and vocal information, worldwide, via the cellphone. From holding to hitchhiking to texting, the thumb has come a long way. Starting now, being "all thumbs" may be more a compliment—thumbs up!—than a criticism, suggesting a deftness in the swift, quiet, social subversion of texting.

Silence and Multitasking

The silence of text is probably its biggest social asset. Whether children should be seen but not heard is debatable. Certainly words are better seen than heard if the sender or receiver wants no one else to know about a communication—also, if others in the environment of the receiver would just as soon not know about it.

The reasons for keeping any communication sub rosa are not usually because the information conveyed is top secret. More likely, the communicator just doesn't want anyone in the vicinity to know that this exchange is taking place. Whether a student in a classroom, an associate at a business meeting, a member of the family at a large gathering, communication without voices allows you to be in two social engagements at once. There is an old Yiddish saying, "With one *tuchus* [rear end] you can't dance at two weddings!" Well, with one texting cellphone, the skillful certainly can manage a word dance at two conversations. At the very least, the people around you assume you are part of their group, while you "text" with someone else on the cellphone.

There is no doubt a whiff of dishonesty about this, to the extent that the people in your physical group are misled into thinking you are paying thorough attention to them. On the other hand, if the multitasking texter is adept, he or she actually may be able to participate, more or less effectively, in the classroom, business meeting, or family gathering while tending to the cellphone. And while one might well conclude that the people in the proximate environment are being cheated of the texter's full participation, we need to be clear that this kind of social cheating is not at all like the literal cheating that a student might also try via text messaging with people outside the classroom in order to get help answering questions on an exam.

Further, on the bright side, the silence of text eliminates completely the disruption of the cellphone in theaters, museums, and restaurants, when strangers are obliged to hear your conversation. (Here we have another good example of a remedial medium—texting remedying the vocal intrusiveness of cellphones—and likely to be far more effective in addressing the problem than silly laws, such as the one banning cellphones in New York City theaters.) Only the people who want your attention and possible conversation are short-changed by surreptitious texting. People who do not want to hear your conversation—people for whom your attention or voice is an annoyance—are beneficiaries of your voiceless phone.

And what about you, the person who is texting while other voice communications are swirling around you? Is the student, business associate, family member well served by this new, literally digital (finger) option? Well, the human being is an inherently multitasking organism, as we have seen. Our brains are hard-wired to run our bodies as well as see, hear, smell, taste, touch, think, and feel at the same time. Our minds have been bred by blind evolution to wring sense out of chaos, to see some order in the universe that is otherwise, as William James famously put it more than a century ago, a "big, booming, buzzing confusion." If we can understand enough of a class or business meeting while sending and receiving text messages on a cellphone—if, for example, students who text during lectures can nonetheless do well on tests, without cheating—perhaps we need to revise our expectations of classroom conduct and, more generally, courteous behavior.

The silent word on the cellphone thus makes it easier for us to be both courteous and discourteous, depending on the degree of attention and participation expected of us in the non-cellphonic part of our environment. If the text on the cellphone is instant messaging—conversation via text—our distraction from the environment at hand will likely be more than if the text on the little screen is a Web page or some other passive document. Books, after all, are easier to close and put away than ongoing conversations.

But the availability of libraries on cellphones—or all the non-interactive media of the Web—may be just as revolutionary in its own way as talking with your fingers.

Libraries with Legs

When I was kid, back in the Bronx in the late 1950s, my three favorite vehicles in the street were ice cream trucks (I had a soft spot for Bungalow Bar and its ice cream sandwich), pizza trucks in front of my junior high school (the sauce was far too sharp and the cheese mundane, but it beat anything in the drab cafeteria), and the library on wheels (okay, yes, I admit it, my tastes even as a kid were more than gustatory). There was something thrilling, even miraculous, on a low-key scale, in the library coming right to me, on the corner of the apartment building in which I lived, right near the stoops where I hung out and played ball.

The selection on the truck wasn't much, but I scored a book on the Abominable Snowman. It would be decades before the Internet brought electronic books right into homes, but even that lacked something of the library on wheels, and not just because books online were in phosphor and pixels. It was perhaps because receipt of things in the home was commonplace, and had been since at least the Sears Roebuck catalog at the turn of the twentieth century. And even though the Internet made its deliveries of electronic text instantly, they were still delivered to the home, not the street.

In contrast, the library on wheels—like the ice cream and pizza trucks, and let's add the venerable fruit man, who made a few appearances in my neighborhood on a horse-drawn wagon (believe it or not) in the early 1950s—brought its wares to where I was playing, walking, talking with my friends. Midway between stores I could choose to frequent, and the apartment in which I lived, these vendors on wheels seemed to come out of nowhere, and thus out of the very fabric of the neighborhood or the universe, unbidden, just to serve me.

The cellphone's provision of electronic books and other online items is similarly always in situ, in sync with the walk of life. The capacity to receive any kind of information at any time (this was the breakthrough of the Web) anywhere you may be (this is the special contribution of the cellphone) turns the whole world into a responsive environment—responsive, at least, to what you want to know. Every hand, every pocket, becomes not only a phone booth but an Internet café.

Further, the drawback of the cellphone for conversation, whether speech or text—your accessibility, or capacity to receive a call, as well as make one, anytime, anywhere—does not apply to all the other information you can elect to receive on your cellphone. You can read a book, watch a movie, visit a Web page via cellphone—but no one can therein read, watch, or visit you. (If a site insists on knowing you and your preferences before letting you access it, you always can decide not to.) You are not, in other words, omni-in-touch in such cellphonic excursions, because the touch in the case of non-interactive text and images goes just one way, from you to the text and images, not vice versa. Thus the library on legs of the cellphone—your legs, your wheels—puts you in the driver's seat.

Or, to return to the power of fingers: If texting lets your fingers do the talking, then accessing libraries on the cellphone lets your fingers do the walking, too—while your legs may be actually, physically, walking somewhere else. Years ago, commercials for the Yellow Pages—directories of business phone numbers—invited us to let our "fingers do the walking." But the paper paths those fingers walked through came bound in a thick, cumbersome book that at best could be lugged from one room to another. And the places our fingers walked to in the Yellow Pages were dumb—in today's digital parlance, inert. They did nothing, just stayed there, frozen on the page, when our fingers touched them. In contrast, the places our cellphonic Internet takes us to are smart, alive, and ready to do business, if we like.

The Smart World

In the long run, the capacity to have all information at our fingertips—fingertips connected to feet in motion—may be a more profound benefit of the cellphone than the opportunity it provides to converse with anyone, anytime, anywhere. There are, after all, a rather limited number of people we might want to talk to in any given period of time—an hour, a day, a month, a year. Perhaps under a hundred in a month? No such limit exists on the amount, variety, and depth of information we might need or choose to pursue.

We come from a world that is rather stupid—in the programming sense, unresponsive—regarding our need for information. Most of the time the piece of the world we happen to be occupying might as well be stone, as far as its capacity to provide the information and services we require. (Actually, even stone presumably can yield some geological information of interest and use to someone. So most of the world, most of the time, is for most of us even less forthcoming than stone as a provider of needed information.) Our only recourse is to physically move to a place where the information we seek is available. The Internet is a big improvement over the brick library and its posted hours and the bad weather that may intervene even when the library is open, but even the Internet, absent a Palm Pilot/cellphone, obliges us to be in a room with a computer connection. If we have no reason or need to be in such a room, other than the information portal it provides—if we would rather be outdoors, in no room, or in a room with no computer—then we surely have lost something in the transaction, even though we may have gained information.

The mobile hearth of the cellphone makes that trade-off no longer necessary. It makes anywhere in the world smart—as we saw in Chapter 4, responsive to our requests for information, anytime we may happen to be there.

It's a nice thought, isn't it? Our mere presence in the world smartens it, as long as we have a cellphone. Or, more precisely, our presence in the world always smartened it, in the traditional meaning of the word, but now it also smartens the world in the newer, digital sense of smart cars and smart buildings. Such devices are more responsive, more alive, than their uneducated originals. But the intelligence of smart buildings and smart cars works only in those buildings and cars. The dwelling next door can be a traditional, run-of-the-mill dullard, the car parked in front of it an old jalopy. In contrast, cellphones make the whole world more giving, more living. If this sounds like some kind of gospel song, that is because the effect is that profound.

But metaphors are not easy here. The "intelligence" of smart cars is due not only to programming—or education—but to fundamental construction that gives them the capacity to be programmed. We might say, then, that the intelligence of smart cars and buildings is, like our own human intelligence, the result of both hard-wiring (genetics in us, construction of chips for cars and buildings) and learning (education for us, programming for the smart objects)—nature and nurture, for machine as well as human, except we supply the "nature," the blueprint, the machine.

Mobility and inertness in the smart world are also complex, and vary according to the item or place that is smart, and what makes it that way. Even the smartest building is inert, in that it does not move anywhere. And even the dumbest building has moving parts, if it has an elevator. Even the most benighted car is of course far less inert than any building—cars move, and they are responsive to our touch, or at least their steering wheels and gas pedals and brakes had better be. Indeed, the intelligence of cars can be measured by how much they allow the vehicle to drive based on prior programming, rather than our hands on the wheel and our foot on the pedal and other controls.

The cellphone, however, makes the world smart in a way that is radically different from smart cars and buildings. Like a magic wand that we carry, the cellphone makes any place in the world instantly smart, anyplace we may happen to wave our phone. The cellphone with Internet access makes that place, anyplace we may happen to be with a cellphone, even smarter. The world and its components stay in place; we supply the mobility; the well-connected cellphone supplies the intelligence.

Information on demand everywhere in the smart world also makes the physical environment itself—sunshine, trees, sidewalks, summer breeze, snow flurries—more accessible. Not only are these environments more responsive, they are more available. In the older world that we are leaving behind—the more numb, dumb, less responsive external world—we not only had less access to information outside, we had no access to the external world when we were inside, in pursuit of information. To talk on the telephone at home or in the office, to watch television in the living room, to log on to the Web from the den, meant we were deprived of the outside, except insofar as we might see it through a window. The new capacity to access the Web with the sun on our face finally puts information in its proper place: part of life, part of the world, to be obtained while we're in the real world, not removed from it, unless we prefer it that way.

But speaking of the world, how much of it is able to enjoy these benefits of the cellphone? In the next chapter we look at how the miracle phone has not only blurred the distinction between indoors and outdoors, but erased much of the international digital divide.

Chapter 9
Leapfrogging Landlines and the Digital Divide

The diffusion of new communications media has had a familiar pattern for centuries: the new media first become available to the wealthiest people and nations, then fan out, slowly or quickly, to the rest. The reason for the slower dissemination usually had to do with what engineers and economists call "infrastructure." Telephones required more than just telephones—talking and listening pieces—which were not very expensive. Telephones also required telephone lines, which were costly, in time as well as money, to install. Talk may have been cheap, but the telephone lines needed for such talk, whether hoisted on poles or buried in the ground, were not. Conversation thus required construction.

Radio and television had the advantage of being wireless, and they therefore entered the homes of the populace far more quickly than did telephone. But even television and radio required more than boxes—"sets"—in the home. They also required broadcast and production facilities. The expense of that process—the cost of sending wireless information and, in the case of television, the cost of creating programs with images and sounds—was one of the reasons both radio and television developed into one-way, receiving-only media. Most people could not and still cannot afford the cost of a broadcast tower in the home. It is much more expensive than a television set, a cable connection, or a satellite dish on the roof.

In the early days of any technology, investment in expensive infrastructure is a gamble—say you strung telephone lines, and nobody wanted to talk? The logic of this situation suggested taking the risks in the most populated, affluent areas: big cities in the wealthiest countries. And if the technology succeeded there, it made sense to try it elsewhere.

The great expense of communications infrastructure also had profound political cost. Early printing presses were such big-ticket items to operate that monarchs were the most likely to afford them. This meant that monarchs controlled them, and royal presses became conveyors not of independently reported news but of propaganda. The advent of advertising as a source of revenue for publishers encouraged the press to cut loose from royal purse strings, where possible, and provided the economic foundation for the Jeffersonian view of the press as not only independent of the government, but its watchdog. Progress in printing technology and consequent reduction of costs coincided with the rise of the "common man" in the Jacksonian era a few decades later. More efficient presses sped the advent of magazines, which could be printed when the machinery had finished its book runs earlier than expected. More things to read—books, newspapers, now magazines— meant more readers. By the end of the nineteenth century, literacy rates in America for the first time succeeded the percentage of the literate among the citizenry of ancient Alexandria.

But the separation of media from government took much longer in other parts of the world. In some places not only did the printing press never leave its royal cradle, but it eventually was joined there by radio and television. Radio towers in Nazi Germany and the Soviet Union—the twentieth-century descendants of royal presses—were literally mouthpieces of Hitler and Stalin, who used them with great insight and impact. Churchill and Franklin Delano Roosevelt had similar talent and success with radio, but the robust democratic traditions in England and America kept the power of radio off the totalitarian track. Nonetheless, the BBC or British Broadcasting Company—which, unlike American networks, is quite literally a part of the British government—was restricted in its reporting, by the British government, during the Falklands War in the 1980s. (Not that U.S. governments and the military have not done their best to regulate reporting of U.S. media during wartime. But such attempts have been less than fully effective. And, in any case, evasion, subversion, non-support, and even de facto obstruction of media is not the same as the U.S. government flatly issuing a cease-and-desist order to NBC, CNN, Fox News, CBS, and ABC, which is what the government of Margaret Thatcher did to the BBC about its Falklands coverage. See Chapter 10 in this book for further discussion of media coverage and war, and how the cellphone has revolutionized this aspect of human conduct.)

The personal computer as a word processor, to continue our brief history, was something of an eye-opener in the evolution of media, infrastructure, and decentralization, because it required neither telephone lines nor broadcast towers. It was a self-contained box, which needed only electricity, already widely available. But the PC came with its own baggage—an infrastructure of skills required by the user. In order to use the Apples and IBM PCs of the early 1980s, you had to be doubly literate—you had to read and write, as well as know how to talk to, command, your computer. The first, like electrical power, was already widespread. Children learned to read in public school. And literate parents could help their children before and during this formal educational process. The second was completely the opposite: no one except a few programmers knew how to use computers at the outset. This meant that even when computer literacy slowly began to appear in grade-school curricula, parents usually were not much help. (The initial profusion of computer systems, in which even every computer that used CP/M had somewhat different commands, exacerbated the problem.)

Further, when telecommunication and the Internet came into the picture, the personal computer did require access to telephone lines. This was no problem in the United States, most of Europe, and the technologically developed world, which in the twentieth century had been pretty thoroughly fitted with phonelines. But not so in other parts of the world. Thus, despite its promising beginnings, the personal computer followed much the same difficult road to diffusion as the printing press, telephone, and broadcast media in many countries. The combination of stiff know-how required by everyone and telephone access unavailable in some sections of the globe created groups of haves and have-nots for personal computer and Web use, both within and among countries.

Attempts were made, with some success, to provide personal computers and training to disadvantaged people and nations. But it would take the cellphone to really start leveling the digital divide.

Cheap Talk

From its very inception, talk has had at least two things going for it: it is cheap, and it is easy. Indeed, in its raw, unamplified form, it costs absolutely nothing. It requires nothing in the way of material technology—just vocal chords and air. Even the most primitive writing requires at least three pieces of technology: the writing implement (pen, pencil), the writing substance (ink, lead), and the writing object (wall, papyrus, paper, etc.). In some of the very earliest forms of writing—carving on a wall—the necessary ingredients were reduced to two, the chisel or sharp rock and the wall. But even those two, or at very least the chisel or rock, cost more than a voice box. The chisel had to be made; a suitably sharp rock, at very least, had to be found. If this didn't cost money or its barter equivalent, it surely cost time. Only writing in the sand with one's finger cost the same as speech—and that was only the case if you happened to be already standing on a sandy beach and didn't have to expend time looking for one. And wherever the sand was, the words on it lasted only until the next wave, and this sort of writing didn't work at all on grass, stone, or any kind of hard soil. For that last "medium," some sort of stick or stone was needed, which, again, could well cost a little time to find.

Talk is not only cheap but very easy. As Noam Chomsky detailed so well, we do not even learn to talk in any conventional sense of learning. Rather, we already know how to speak, partially, as we progress into toddlerhood, and talking is elicited, brought forth from us, in much the same way as walking. That's why children tend not to make certain mistakes as they "learn" how to speak. A young child may hear a parent say, "The boy hit the ball." The child may later just say, "Boy hit," or "Boy ball," not "hit the"—this is because the child apparently has some innate, genetically provided sense of subject, verb, object, and even definite article sufficient for the child to know that "hit the" or "the hit" is in no way an approximation of "the boy hit the ball." What children hear at first is not a bewildering babble of unrelated words, but a weave they can connect to, discern significant components of, as they begin to put together their own language. When they first hear "the boy hit the ball," they may well not understand the specific meaning of the words, but they grasp something essential of the relationship of those words to one another, and how they connect to real actions in the world. And they grasp this years before they can consciously study and talk about such relationships—well before they learn grammar in school.

Of course, the vocabulary part of speech—the defined meaning of each word, provided by the language or, more generally, the society—is undoubtedly learned, but even this is taught more easily, effortlessly, than the operation of any other medium, except perhaps turning on a television. Children pick up words spoken by parents and family; they do it just by living, without particularly trying. They go to school for much more exacting education when learning how to read and write, and no doubt acquire some additional vocabulary and a grammatical pointer or two for speech in the bargain. But no one learns how to speak in school, in the sense of uttering

understandable sentences. On that basic level of verbal perfor-
mance, kids come to kindergarten already well spoken.

And if they do not get to kindergarten or school, no matter.
Kids, people, all human beings of all cultures speak (unless they
have a physical or mental impediment). If it thinks, it almost
always speaks. If it speaks, it almost always thinks. (The exception here might be the parrot, but that's really mimicry, not
speech. Machines that speak do so as a result of thinking—
ours.) Words are different, sounds are different, but their
central role in human affairs is the same all over the world.

This ease and inexpense of speech accounts for the success
of the telephone over the telegraph. Indeed, inasmuch as the
telephone utilized poles and wire paths already constructed for
the telegraph, Samuel Morse's invention carried with it the
seeds of its own displacement by Alexander Graham Bell's. But
the cost of additional poles and wires nonetheless slowed the
telephone's growth. The cellphone requires neither.

Cellphones do require either land-based towers or satellites to
relay conversations. But the towers cost about $30,000 to con-
struct, a fraction of the price of poles and wires. And satellites
are available for renting. (There are more than 26,000 satellites
currently in the sky.) In both knowledge base and technology,
cellphones require the least infrastructure—or the infrastructure
with the least expense of money and time—in history, after
speech. But the gap between the prerequisites of speech and cellphone is of course nonetheless enormous: we come equipped to
speak, but many areas of the world and even the United States
still lack complete cellphone coverage, which is why there are so
many holes and dead pockets in service. The relatively low
expense of cellphone infrastructure, however, means that these
holes and pockets are likely to be filled quickly.

Leapfrogging

The French phone system used to be a dismal embarrassment.
A National Assemblyman observed, several decades after

World War II, that "half of France is waiting for a telephone, the other half is waiting for a dial tone." But just a few years later, by the mid-1980s, the "Minitel" system had transformed France into one of the most advanced telecommunicating nations on Earth. Instead of printing and distributing massive telephone directories, which required revision and therefore new printing and distribution every year, the French government decided to distribute computer terminals through which citizens could access telephone numbers. This took advantage of the infinite refreshability of the computer screen—on which an unlimited number of phone numbers could be printed, until the computer itself broke down—in contrast to the single set of numbers wedded forever to the printed paper page, and thus the pages in a telephone book. Although a computer terminal cost more than a printed directory, this investment in infrastructure soon paid off and had consequences that went far beyond looking for phone numbers.

The Minitel system also allowed exchange of text messages, and soon "hot chatting" (as it was then called), practiced by a few hundred thousand subscribers on CompuServe and similar online networks in the United States, became a national pastime in France. First denounced and then embraced by *Le Monde* and other guardians of French culture, the "messagerie rose" became a way of life for French in the night, who undressed each other and made love via text. France had leapfrogged into the twenty-first century of texting and instant messaging—indeed, had arrived here about fifteen years early. Except nowadays, not only do people text about sex and lots of other things throughout the day, but pornographic e-mails average about 2.5 billion worldwide daily (according to Family Safe Media's "Pornography Statistics," 2003). As in the heyday of Victorian photography, and the carefully sequenced photographs by Marey and Muybridge of nude women walking down staircases that led to the invention of motion pictures, sex once again pointed the way for media.

But the French feat of course also required some preexisting infrastructure of phone lines. It could not have occurred, back then, in an undeveloped part of the world. But it could today, via wireless cell technology, and the principle of leapfrogging it embodies remains the same.

Leapfrogging is possible because, contrary to the usual pattern of technological diffusion, sometimes new media, or crucial components of new media operations, can be less expensive, and thus easier to adopt and disseminate, than older media. The Ayatollah Khomeini's fundamentalist Islamic revolution in Iran in the late 1970s used audiocassettes to distribute its messages to an illiterate population. On the other hand, the Soviet Union was not able to keep up with the American computer revolution in the 1980s. It's all in the cost: cassettes cost a lot less to produce than computers, and require no literacy or other skills to operate.

Cellphones these days cost about as much as cassettes did then. No wonder cellphone use is growing faster than the capacity of cellphone networks—not only in the United States and technologically advanced societies such as Japan and Western Europe, but all over the world. As far as the cellphone is concerned, just about everywhere is technologically advanced.

Pick a name of any nation, and search for it in conjunction with cellphones on Yahoo. I tried Kenya in late 2002 and found a report from July 2002, which explained that Safaricom, one of Kenya's two leading cellphone providers, was being sued by its subscribers because of its congested networks. Safaricom acknowledged that its capacity for 500,000 users was close to being filled, with 440,000 subscribers. It ordered expansion of its network, which would increase its capacity to 750,000.

I checked Kenya and cellphones again on Yahoo in early 2003. Safaricom and its rival, KenCell, had nearly 1.3 million cellphone subscribers. By the time you're reading this, that number will no doubt be much higher. Nick Wachira's "Wireless in Kenya Takes a Village" (2003) offers then-current details. Wachira and experts quoted in his article attribute the explosive growth to "Kenyans lov[ing] to talk" and deep-rooted community "conviviality." The more apt point, I think, is that most human beings love to talk, which is why cellphone services are bursting at the seams everywhere in the world. (See Howard Rheingold's *Smart Mobs*, 2003, for discussion of cellphones and their social impact in Japan, the Philippines, and elsewhere.)

The good news about these growing pains is that increases in carrying capacity are relatively easy to come by, because of the low cost of infrastructure discussed above. A given company, of course, may miscalculate and go out of business. But the cellphone as a mode of conversation, text messaging, and Web access will not.

Further, every increase in cellphone use and infrastructure anyplace in the world is a win for everyone else in the world: the increase helps not only the people in the given region, but anyone else in the world who would like to contact someone in that region or visit in person. As far as access goes—and except insofar as access can be an intrusion, as when you do not want to be reached—every new cellphone is a win/win/win . . . and so forth, situation, exponentially extending to every person in this world with a cellphone.

Cellphonic Passports for Global Travelers

Up until the advent of the cellphone, to travel to another part of the world usually meant, if not being out of touch, being obliged to communicate through an unfamiliar phone or computer system. The cellphone allows world travelers to communicate on their own terms and equipment.

Back in the 1960s, Marshall McLuhan observed that electronic media were changing the world of disparate communities into a "global village." At that time, what this global village amounted to was everyone in the same country watching the same thing at the same time on television (or hearing the same thing on radio). Admittedly, this was far more unified a community than people reading newspapers and books at their own times and paces and occasions, or even going to the movies in lots of separate groups at lots of different times and places to see a similar handful of movies.

In succeeding years, satellites and world news networks such as CNN turned the regular national audience into an international one. Prior to the rise of cable/satellite television, only rare television events like the Super Bowl, the Academy Awards, and the marriage of Charles and Diana were seen everywhere in the world at once. But the cabled global village was still a strange one—a village of spectators, with everyone unmoving, in their seats, and unable to talk to anyone else in the global or national village, unless he or she happened to be seated right next to you, or happened to be in your home, or unless you were willing to make an expensive, multi-dollar telephone call (which is what international and even interstate calls cost in those days) to someone watching the same TV show someplace else in the world.

The Internet finally gave the global villagers the power of inexpensive, easy conversation—world denizens could now see the same thing on television and then discuss it with any-one else in the world who happened to be online (via instant messaging) or had e-mail. Television had given the global vil-lagers eyes and ears; the Web gave them tongues, expressed for the most part through fingers. And the Web, as a medium of pictures and text, also could be the source of news and events that world villagers wanted to talk about. (I first found out about the death of Princess Diana on the Web, in a live online chat I was having about the Hugo science fiction awards, which were being announced that evening.)

But the villagers were still stuck to their seats. And this kept the global village more like a global stadium. The cellphone at last gets the crowd out of their seats, on to their feet, and into the world—if not necessarily cheering, at least in physical reality, in realspace, as well as in cyberspace. (See my

Realspace: The Fate of Physical Presence in the Digital Age, On and Off Planet, 2003, for more on the benefits of interacting in "realspace"—the physical world—rather than in cyberspace.) And this physical reality, in the case of the cellphone, is coming to mean anywhere in the world. The cellphone is thus a passport to the rest of the world, not only figuratively, as when we take it with us for a walk in Central Park in New York City and we wish to be in touch with someone in Hyde Park in London, but more literally, when we take it with us for a trip overseas and wish to be in touch with people— and Web sites—we visited back home.

Years ago I saw a news story on a local TV station about a group of masonry workers, from the People's Republic of China, who were invited to New York City to do some very specialized renovation work on an old cathedral. These people were apparently the only workers in the world who still had the venerable skills needed to do the job. They spoke no English and had never been out of their country before. The person who arranged for the invitation explained that as long as the workers would be able to eat their customary food— shipped to them in New York from China, specially for the occasion—they would be content, and not feel too homesick or uncomfortable in their strange, new surroundings.

For many people, being in touch with customary information and people is at least as important as food. On the one hand, we sometimes travel to get away from the ordinary in our lives, to have some time away from our usual locale. On the other hand, we like it in easy reach nonetheless, so as not to feel too dislocated. In this matter of being not home and home at the same time, the cellphone allows us to eat our cake and still have it—as the cellphone does with so many aspects of communication.

In North America, the telegraph poles that sprang up alongside railroad tracks made migration to the West more attractive. To leave one's family back East was not to leave it entirely. Although telegraph and telephone service has long been available worldwide, it by and large did not keep up, prior to the cellphone, with the digital revolution in the last decades of the twentieth century. Phone calls charged to credit cards, and local nodes for computer connections, helped somewhat, but to travel overseas was still to be in a state of information deprivation, in which you were cut off from at least some of your usual sources of information and conversation.

The cellphone in the world traveler's hand may finally change that. One of the most far-reaching legacies of the cellphone may be that it finally brought the active, flesh-and-blood global village into being, by cushioning travel to any part of that village with access to any and all desired information. Long after the ring in the restaurant ceases to be an annoyance, we may be reaping the opportunities of the cellphone's world community.

But as with all things technological, with all new developments in evolution, we need to be alert to potential drawbacks of a world community more fully realized through the cellphone and its easy conversation. As in the biological world, diversity in human culture has great value as a source of innovation and historical connection. A different way of doing things, another way of thinking, can serve as checks and balances on the dominant mode, even insurance in case it fails. What we want, ideally, from global community is a world in which heterogeneity is more comfortably sampled, not completely melted into a homogeneity in which everything and everyone is the same.

And world community is not necessarily the same as world peace. In general, exchange of information can clarify differences, and it can even avert or reduce hostilities. The Battle of New Orleans, for example, was fought in 1814 after the War of 1812 between the United States and Britain had been concluded with a peace treaty in Paris. But no one in America knew about the treaty, because the telegraph was still decades away, and the transatlantic telegraph even further. But information also can facilitate military action—which may be good, if the opponent is deserving of forceful attention. Historians agree that the Allied cracking of the German Enigma code by Alan Turing (also responsible for the Turing machine, which helped set the theoretical basis for modern computing and the digital revolution, and the Turing test, which helped set criteria for whether artificial intelligence is truly, humanly intelligent) hastened and perhaps made inevitable the Nazi defeat in World War II by giving the Allies details of German military plans—sometimes ahead of German generals in the field.

In the next chapter we consider the cellphone at war.

Chapter 10
The Cellphone at War

New media have been shaping the public's perception of war ever since Mathew Brady began photographing the Civil War. For the first time in history, people not present at military camps and battlefields could see, literally, what war was like— not descriptions, not paintings, but actual images captured by the lenses, the surrogate eyes, of cameras. Photographs had been taken of the Crimean War in the 1850s, but Brady's extensive photographs of the American Civil War in the following decade were decisive in opening theaters of war to public view. Receiving permission, but no funding, from Abraham Lincoln to follow and photograph the Union Army, Brady fielded dozens of photographers who took eight thousand negatives, all as a commercial enterprise. The haunting faces and demeanors of soldiers captured by Brady's photographers before and after battles fascinated patrons of his gallery on the corner of Fulton Street and Broadway in New York City, far from the battlefields, for years. The faces were truly, as French film theorist André Bazin would note about the essence of photography nearly a century later, images rescued from their "proper corruption" in time.

But even the most rapidly, lavishly published or displayed photograph was thin, frozen, and seen well after the battle was over. Almost a century later, newsreels that ran at the beginning of motion picture shows during World War II offered more full-bodied, kinetic coverage, but were subject to similar delay. The Vietnam War was on television in the living rooms of Americans in the 1960s less than a day after events in the field, but even this was less than immediate, live coverage.

Light travels faster than sound as a form of energy, but sound always had the historical advantage over images when it came to speed of long-distance communication. Telephone and radio thus conveyed speech decades before there were images in telecommunication. Edward R. Murrow's famous radio broadcasts from London during World War II were live. "This is London," Murrow would begin, in a tone that spoke of a world hanging in the balance, which it was, as German bombs fell all around him. But his was a medium conveying only the sound of events whose visual aspect—what the bombing actually looked like—was enormously important. And London was just a single theater in a far-flung multiplex of world war. The radio broadcasts of Murrow and others, breathtaking at the time, were not yet quite the public's ears on war as a whole, and not at all its eyes.

By the time of the first Gulf War in 1991, technology had developed for what we today call "streaming"—live, immediate, continuous—coverage. And more than four decades of audiovisual refinement, in television and video, made this coverage multidimensional. But the equipment was highly expensive and clunky by current standards, and the military was determined to carefully control media reporting of that war. (A widely held view among advocates of the Vietnam War was that the war was lost because adverse television coverage undermined American support. I would argue that the war was lost because, unlike the Iraqi War, the Vietnam War had weak moral grounding. The United States was intervening in a civil war. The leader of North Vietnam, Ho Chi Minh, had no tradition of using weapons of mass destruction. And, most important, the war against international communism of which the Vietnam War was a part had no equivalent of the events of September 11, 2001, and thus in this crucial aspect was unlike the war on terrorism. No communist state or guerrilla group had ever killed three thousand civilians in one morning on American soil. In other words, the problem in Vietnam was neither the media nor the military, but the mission. And the

media, if anything, took far too long to begin critical examination of the war. Walter Cronkite, for example, on CBS-TV,
was in general favorably disposed toward the Vietnam War
until the Tet Offensive in January 1968. But that's a story for
another book.)

The ironic result of the enhanced but restricted media
coverage of the first Gulf War, despite the advent of CNN as
an all-news cable station and the twenty-four-hour reporting it
provided, was that most of this war was fought off the screen,
and thus beyond public viewing. Military summaries from
command central in Saudi Arabia, supplemented by bird's-eye
views from the tips of smart missiles that looked more like virtual reality than real war, were about the closest that viewers
back home got to the front lines. Although just about everyone was happy with the ejection of Iraq from Kuwait at the
end of that war, the media with all of their high-tech advantages got less than universal acclaim. The troops on the
ground felt that their story had not been told, that their work
had been invisible to the public—the military later lamented
that few had seen the individual acts of heroism—and, for
many in America, the war seemed like a big video game.

All of that would change in the second war against Iraq.

The Cellphonic Journalist

The opening days of the war against Iraq in March 2003 were
distinguished not only by revolutionary weapons technology—
missiles that could fly through specific windows of buildings,
from launches hundreds of miles away, and whose error mar-
gins were measured in inches—but by comparably extraordinary communications equipment. Live coverage of the
bombing of Baghdad and live reports from journalists
"embedded" in tank columns moving through the deserts of
Iraq provided unprecedented windows on war, in living rooms,
bedrooms, and bars all over the world. The spark-plug of all

this, the key conduit that made it happen, was the cellphone, with its mobile videophone and satellite connections.

In retrospect, the cellphone was an ideal instrument for reportage of war—if it hadn't been invented and developed already, it might have been, just for that purpose. The cellphone is small, self-contained, live, and interactive. Of course it requires external relaying facilities—dedicated satellites provide clearer, but less frequently available, connections than conventional "cells" (which use a combination of land relays locally and more general satellites internationally). And a television station (cable, network, or local) has to present what is reported through the cellphone to the public. But once these connections are in place, the cellphonic reporter becomes the most powerful, knowledgeable journalist in the history of war, able to convey events, to comment on them, to answer questions about them from a news anchor or anyone the TV news program permits, literally as the events are happening.

The addition of the videophone—transforming the cellphone into the video-cellphone—at last made the front-line, embedded reporter truly the public's eyes as well as ears. The long, uneven, twentieth-century history of the videophone—which, despite its early appearance, has yet to become as fully accepted as the telephone before it and the cellphone after it—is a fascinating tale in itself, which we will explore in the next chapter. Here we can note that war, as it often does, not only encourages the invention of new weapons and the recruitment of nascent technologies, but in this case pulled from the sidelines the videophone, hovering for decades on the edge of public adoption, and made it a crucial player in the reporting from deserts, battle scenes, and city streets. Conventional video (not video-cellphone) through satellite uplinks provided some excellent, crystal-clear coverage. A variety of video, satellite, and cellphonic connections, used by various reporters in various situations, delivered images of varying technical quality throughout the war. But the best equipment required at least fifteen or more minutes to deploy, unlike the grainy video-cellphone, which could be brought into service almost instantly.

The equipment of reporting in the Iraqi War—in short, the cellphone and its adjuncts—was thus a consolidation and culmination of wartime media beginning with the photograph and proceeding through motion photography, radio, and television. (The telegraph, invented around the same time as photography, also played its historical role, beginning, like the photograph, with the Crimean and American Civil wars. But telegrams were vehicles of communication between officers, between presidents and generals—such as Lincoln and Grant—and between reporters and editors. The public came later, after the telegrams, when the results of these communiqués were published in newspapers.)

But media in general—all media, but media of reporting in particular—are ultimately only as effective as the people who use them to convey information. A revolution requires more than unprecedented equipment. It requires people who understand how to make the most of the equipment—as Mathew Brady and his cadre of Civil War photographers did—even though the technology was not readily or completely available before.

The cadre of embedded journalists in the 2003 Iraqi War ranged from old hands like Ted Koppel (with Vietnam reporting experience, and, due to his ABC-TV *Nightline* show, among the best-known news anchors since Walter Cronkite) to Dan Dahler, a relative unknown, also with ABC-TV News. All of the major news outlets had "embeds," outfitted with various kinds of cellphones, videophones, and video hookups to satellites above. NBC's David Bloom, who died of a pulmonary embolism in the desert, on the job, worked out of his "Bloom-mobile," a refurbished tank that he had helped design. The camera was so well mounted that it produced clear, stable images—relayed to a transmission truck and then to NBC in New York via satellite—even with the tank moving along at a bumpy fifty miles per hour.

But how good were the embedded, cellphonic journalists in covering the story—the immediate heat of war—on live, global television?

Embedded Reporters with Cellphones

One journalistic advantage of the inextricable (though diminishing) delay of photography, motion pictures, and television as conveyors of wartime news is that the delay worked to the benefit of one of the cardinal goals of journalism: objectivity. Although rapid delivery of news was also a goal, this was not supposed to be done at the expense of the journalist's detachment from the story. An old-fashioned photograph, which could easily take days or longer to reach the public in the nineteenth century, provided ideal conditions for detachment and separation of reporting from actual events. Yet, on occasion, this separation could still work against the best practice of journalism, and not because of government intervention.

The telegraph conveyed information immediately, but newspapers still required time to print the telegraphic accounts. William Randolph Hearst's infamous alleged advice to his reporters in Cuba in 1897 prior to the start of the Spanish–American War—"You furnish the pictures, I'll furnish the war"—shows the potential for manipulation of news delayed, processed through intermediate editors and publishers. (According to Emery and Emery's *The Press and America*, 1992, there is no proof that Hearst actually sent this telegram. We just have the assertion of Hearst reporter James Creelman, in his 1901 account, *On the Great Highway*. Creelman was in Cuba, working for Hearst at the time, along with Richard Harding Davis, another reporter, and artist Frederic Remington, who Creelman says cabled Hearst that the war was not going to occur. But as Emery and Emery remark, whether true or not, this story "reflected the situation.") The lesson of the Hearst-Remington episode—real or apocryphal—is that separation from unfolding events, the fat of delay, was not always healthy for journalism. Sometimes it resulted in the public getting a story that was far less true than if the news had been conveyed immediately, firsthand, with no editor intermediaries. (On yet another hand, Jayson Blair's transgressions at the *New York Times*, which came to light in 2003, clearly resulted from not enough editorial supervision. See a few paragraphs below for more on Blair and the *New York Times*.)

The first undelayed, unprocessed reporting of news—war and otherwise—awaited radio. Lewis Mumford, as we saw in Chapter 5, distrusted the immediacy of radio. He first expressed his misgivings in 1934 (in *Technics and Civilization*), prior to Murrow's broadcasts in World War II. But Mumford repeated them in *The Pentagon of Power* in 1970, indeed quoting from his 1934 warning that immediate communication hastens "mass reactions." Mumford was talking about radio—and then radio and television—in general, not just in war reporting. (Hitler certainly made ample use of radio to stir up the German public. He had earlier indicated in *Mein Kampf*, 1924, his distrust of journalists and their penchant for distorting his views in their reporting. Hitler preferred, instead, talking directly to the German people— possible for groups only the size of rallies prior to radio, possible nationwide after radio.) But Mumford's concerns about immediacy being at odds with objective, rational analysis would seem to have the most relevance to reporting in the actual heat of battle, with bullets flying as fast as words.

And yet the war journalists of traditional radio and television usually were far more removed from their public—the immediate radio reporting of Murrow, of the bombs falling around him, would be a partial exception—than the video-cellphonic, embedded journalist. Indeed, if we were to place all journalists—print, photographic, radio, TV, cellphonic—into one of two groups, based on immediacy of coverage, then the cellphonic would be in one group, and all of the other journalists in the other. Most radio broadcasts, after all, like most television and all newspapers, report events that already happened. For that matter, so, too, do most reporters—and Web loggers—on the Internet.

How did these unique kinds of old and young, famous and unknown, cellphonic journalists perform?

As of this writing (December 2003), there is not a single known case in which an embedded journalist's reporting was distorted by his or her immediate access to the world at large—not a single case in which access to a cellphone in hand resulted in a mishandling or distortion of the facts or the truth at hand. (A cellphone apparently assisted in a serious disfigurement of journalism by a reporter covering a major, earlier story in America. Jayson Blair filed fictitious reports in the *New York Times* about the Washington, D.C., sniper case—claiming to be on the scene, but really calling in from his cellphone in Brooklyn, New York. He later fabricated an interview with the father of Jessica Lynch, the American soldier rescued from a hospital behind enemy lines. But these deceptions were the result of careful planning, not distortions made in the fury of immediate war coverage via cellphone.)

Peter Arnett did give an unfortunate interview to Iraqi TV in the early days of the war, saying the American coalition war plan was not working. But this was a traditional radio interview, which could have been conducted sixty years ago. Arnett was working for MSNBC and *National Geographic* at the time. They promptly fired him. (I commented on a local New York TV news show that Arnett was entitled to talk on any radio station he pleased, but he was certainly not entitled to continue being employed, under those circumstances, by the American media that were paying him to be in Baghdad.) The *Daily Mirror* of London promptly hired him.

Geraldo Rivera was asked by the U.S. Pentagon to leave Iraq after he drew a diagram in the sand on live TV (Fox News Channel) indicating the coalition's plan of attack for Baghdad.

Rivera, technically, was not an embedded reporter (he had not gone through "embed" training, and was not attached to a specific unit)—but his report was disturbing nonetheless because, if correct, it could have jeopardized the lives of coalition troops. But, significantly, although this incident was a notable failure of wartime reporting (assuming that Rivera's information was accurate), it was not a failure to be objective or to report the truth. In fact, it was failure precisely because of the opposite: it reported too much of the truth. (This has always been the military's concern about wartime reporting: it could jeopardize lives. American media usually have understood this completely and voluntarily have refrained from divulging information that could be dangerous to troops or to any Americans in life-threatening situations. When Iran held Americans hostage in the late 1970s, for example, American media did not reveal that several Americans hiding out in the Canadian embassy in Tehran were given forged Canadian passports, which they used to leave the country safely. Knowledge of this might well have angered the Iranians, which could have jeopardized the lives of the Americans still in captivity. The first report of this came out in a Canadian newspaper, while the hostages were still in Iran; fortunately, no one was hurt as a result.)

Sanjay Gupta, a neurosurgeon embedded as a CNN journalist with the "Devil Docs" (a military medical unit), is the only embedded reporter whose objectivity was ever questioned during the war. The issue arose when he put down his cellphone and performed emergency surgery on a severely injured two-year-old Iraqi boy. (The child died, notwithstanding Gupta's efforts.) "I knew I was going into a place where people were going to be injured," Gupta said in a subsequent interview in the New York Daily News (see Richard Huff, 2003). "I didn't volunteer for this. I made it quite clear my mission was journalism, not medicine." But can a journalist objectively report on a story in which he or she is one of the main participants?

"I do think a journalist being objective and detached from the story is a very, very important goal," I said, when interviewed for the same story. "But it's not more important than life itself." In other words, sometimes the story, the goal of journalism, is not the most important thing. A poorly reported story can be corrected; a death cannot. There are no errata listings in the great hereafter.

So, on the human level—on the most important level—I think Dr. Gupta did the right thing, and he deserves not criticism but commendation. But even in the more narrow realm of reporting, we need to note that he did nothing wrong. He did not, as far as we know, intentionally or otherwise distort the information he presented throughout his war coverage. At worst, his re-donning of surgical scrubs potentially put him in a position where his reporting might have suffered. Real benefits are always worth pursuing at the expense of hypothetical damages—even when the benefits are not realized or even when they are not matters of life and death.

As war stories emerge in the years ahead, we may yet learn of some embedded reporter, somewhere, whose lightning-quick reports in the thick of a battle, whose journalism in the midst of comrades who ate and slept and risked their lives along with this reporter, resulted in compromised reporting. But as of now, such diminishment of the journalistic ideal must be counted as but a negative potential, not a reality, and reckoned alongside of the extraordinary, continuous, live coverage of the war provided by embedded journalists with cellphones.

The Unembedded, Unprotected Journalist

Embedded journalists were not the only reporters who brought the 2003 Iraqi War to the world via video-cellphone.

In the early morning of April 13, 2003, New York time—it was eight hours later, in the early light of day in Iraq—Brent Sadler began what would be one of the most remarkable, live-televised journeys of the war. He saw no battles, bomb raids, or even skirmishes. But his three hours with a video-cellphone told an unfolding story as harrowing as I have ever seen. Indeed, more so, because it was happening in real time, right in front of my eyes, right there on television, and I had no idea how it would end.

Sadler was an unembedded journalist working for CNN. This meant that he was not attached to any military unit. The advantage of this arrangement was that he could go where he pleased, pursue a story wherever it led him. The downside was that he had no military protection. He and his unit—a convoy of six trucks, including one with a satellite dish for uplink, in case they had time to set it up (otherwise he could use his video-cellphone)—were on their own.

Here in New York, I sat down and turned on the television shortly after midnight. I had intended to take a brief break from writing this book—I had just finished most of the "Embedded Reporters" section you have just read. I flipped through the cable news stations and stopped on CNN.

Sadler and his group were in the vicinity of Tikrit, the hometown of Saddam Hussein, and the last place in Iraq of any military significance not in coalition hands at that time. Sadler's group had camped in a concealed area overnight, he explained, so they would be safe both from Saddam loyalists and from coalition air strikes that might have mistaken Sadler and his crew for Fedayeen, the Iraqi irregulars. Now that it was light out, Sadler was looking to see how close he could get to Tikrit—perhaps even the center of town. He told us this on his cellphone, with videophone providing shaky images of the countryside as he and his convoy moved out. The road was mostly deserted, certainly of any Iraqi military and apparently— Sadler hoped—of anyone with hostile intentions.

Sadler took us to an abandoned Republican Guard strong-hold, with a statue of Saddam at the entrance and a red trian-gle (the Guard insignia) on the wall. Back on the road, Sadler mounted an abandoned tank and told us the machine gun in the turret still had ammunition. The videophone showed us all of this, as well as various people and vehicles that were now moving along the road, all presumably Iraqi civilian, moving the other way, opposite and passing Sadler's little convoy, out of Tikrit.

Sadler and his interpreter talked to some of them. "Saddam hallah Tikrit," we heard the Iraqis say. "Saddam is finished in Tikrit," Sadler provided the translation.

At this point, Sadler pondered his next move. The problem was that, although there were no identifiably Iraqi military or Fedayeen fighters where he was, they could be around the next bend. And there were no coalition forces around, either. He decided to stop a few miles outside of Tikrit and try to gain more information from people leaving the city. He disconnected his sound equipment and left the videophone camera in his vehicle, so as not to intimidate his interview subjects.

Soon he returned to his vehicle, hooked up the sound and the image, and informed us that he had spoken to an Iraqi teacher—one Fayed—who had said that Tikrit was safe. Fayed had offered to guide Sadler into the city.

Sadler decided to accept the offer. His vehicle followed Fayed's. Most of the rest of the convoy stayed put. On the words crawling beneath the image on my screen from Sadler's videophone, I saw, "Centcom jokes that CNN takes Tikrit. . . ." Anderson Cooper, the CNN anchor who was keeping in constant touch with Sadler, reminded us that the coalition forces had not yet taken Tikrit, as far as anyone knew.

Sadler had told us earlier that what he was most concerned about was coming upon a still-operative Iraqi enemy checkpoint—they might not take kindly to Western reporters. Now his vehicle approached just such a place.

Arabic shouting . . . the video screen goes black . . .

But moments later the video is back on, and Sadler tells us that the Iraqis at the checkpoint did not want to be on television. Camera shy. Apparently there were no other problems. Sadler's vehicle starts moving forward again. . . .

At some point, I realize that there have been no commercial interruptions for a while. This is the most amazing *un*television I have ever seen—because it is more than television, it is video-cellphone television, supported by a network, CNN, that has the understanding to let it play out, unpunctured by ads for toothpaste. (The media theorist part of my brain notes somewhere that this may be the birth of a genuinely new medium. The aftermath of the JFK assassination, 9/11, and other catastrophic events also have been given commercial-free coverage. But Brent Sadler's video-conveyed journey into the heart of darkness is just low-key, wee-hour-of-the-morning reporting of no particular event in a war that is apparently almost over.)

But now Sadler's vehicle is stopping again. Sound and image go off. Anderson Cooper provides a summary for those who might have just tuned in. Sadler gets reconnected and explains that these Iraqis, minor officials or military of some sort, want him to go to Ba'ath Party headquarters in Tikrit to get permission to proceed.

"And I assume you're not going to follow that advice," Cooper says.

Certainly not, Sadler replies, and explains that his vehicle will be turning around and leaving—going back the way they came—as quickly as possible.

There is a subtle but unmistakable change in Sadler's attitude, his tone of voice, at this point. Previously tense and clipped, it now speaks, without explicitly saying so, of imminent, even deadly danger. For the viewer at home, the video-cellphonic live television is turning from riveting to harrowing. (I had thought I wanted to get a glass of orange juice before sitting down at the television. I'm still in the mood for it, but I don't want to risk even a second away from the screen.)

Sadler's vehicle, retracing its path, now arrives at the first checkpoint—the place where, a minute or so earlier, Sadler had been greeted with demands that he shut off his camera. Now he's greeted with something else.

We hear gunfire—rapid machine gun fire. (It sounds like popcorn popping.) "We're under attack, under attack," Sadler says quietly, breathlessly. My heart is pounding. I can all too easily imagine the worst. "We're okay," Sadler says a moment later.

He explains that his security guard—I'm pretty sure this is the first we heard of him—returned fire. "We shot our way through," Sadler says. But they're not home free, by any means. The videophone is rolling. Sadler says that this is the first time, in all his years of reporting, that he has ever come under fire. He says his worst-case scenario is happening.

Now Sadler tells us that a vehicle is attempting to pull up alongside his.

"Is it hostile?" Cooper asks.

"Yes," Sadler replies.

More gunfire. "We're under fire," he says. It's small arms, not machine guns, this time. (I recall hearing, years earlier, a replay of the last desperate words of a local traffic reporter trapped in a helicopter going down in the Hudson River. She didn't survive the crash. I don't want the live Sadler report to be dèja-vu.)

But Sadler's vehicles outrun this second attack—not before the back windows are shot out of one of his trucks, however, and his producer is wounded.

They reunite with the other vehicles in the CNN convoy and drive down the road, away from Tikrit. "We're going seventy miles an hour," Sadler says. And soon the video-cellphone connection is lost.

Television News Comes into Its Own Due to the Cellphone

Sadler and his crew survived. A military analyst commented shortly after on CNN that Sadler's reporting was one of the most extraordinary things he had ever seen. He added that this is what can happen when journalists proceed without military accompaniment into hostile territory.

The analyst was right on both counts. Interestingly, with all the attention given to embedded journalists—and their coverage was extraordinary—it was an unembedded journalist, unprotected, unscripted, who provided the most extraordinary coverage of the war. It was in those moments of unexpected, vulnerable reporting—just a journalist with his equipment (and one security guard)—that the cellphone and the video-phone achieved their epitome in wartime journalism.

Television, of course, played a crucial role in this as well—without CNN's televised hookup, no one would have seen or heard this. And, looked at in another way, Brent Sadler's reporting on this day in particular, and the cellphonic coverage of the war through television in general, can be seen as a coming of age, a fruition, at last, of television and its potential as a journalistic medium.

I say "at last" because, as a medium of live, breathtaking news, television until the Iraqi War had never equaled what Edward R. Murrow had done on radio. Just as some film critics had lamented that "talking" motion pictures beginning with Al Jolson's *The Jazz Singer* had lost some of the quiet, balletic beauty of silent movies, so had devotees of radio journalism noticed that news on television was missing something. The reason, in both cases, was the cumbersome nature of the new equipment. Talking motion pictures required big microphones, which got in the way of smooth movement of cameras and shots. (They still can get in the way. Every once in a while, in a low-budget movie, you can spot a microphone protruding into the top of the scene.) Television required huge cameras—even bigger than the big microphones of radio and movies—which made immediate, fast-moving coverage very difficult. Instead, most news on television, including during wartime, consisted of talking heads in seats, on panels. The big innovation during the first Gulf War was that some of the talking heads were retired colonels and generals rather than news anchors and reporters, and they were standing, not sitting (this last also due, in part, to the streamlining of microphones).

Seen in this light, the video-cellphone came to the rescue of television news and enabled it finally to live up to its potential. Ironically, in the 1920s television first emerged out of attempts to create a telephone with pictures, or videophone. Now, due to the cellphone, the videophone has reunited with television, found a niche that permits us to see and hear events anywhere in the world.

When media historians look back at the Iraqi War, they will no doubt observe that it was then that television first became part of the cellphone revolution. Like the Internet, the future of television news may well reside in the cellphone. (Indeed, in the fall of 2003, the first cellphones with television reception were marketed.)

Cellphones vs. War Blogs

The cellphone with its video attachment was not the only new medium to make its debut during the Iraqi, or second Gulf, War. Numerous people obtained their information through war "blogs"—Web logs—devoted to firsthand, personal accounts and commentary on the war, available on the Internet. As is the case with everything on the Web, the salient adjective regarding these blogs is "personal"—meaning direct from the heart or head, unmediated—since such postings need not obtain the prior approval and refinement of editors and producers. On the Internet, the writer, editor, and producer are often the same person.

The Iraqi War actually was not the first time the Internet was used for such unfiltered communications. Students in Tiananmen Square in China in 1989 sent e-mail to readers in the West. With all other media controlled or, in the case of Western journalists, obstructed by Chinese authorities, at that time the Internet provided the only possible source of untainted information out of China. (Earlier in the protests, television cameras recorded vivid scenes in Beijing, the most memorable being the student standing up to the oncoming tank. It was the broadcast of such devastating—to Chinese authorities—images all around the world that led the Chinese government to crack down on TV journalists. The Internet took up the slack. Chinese authorities were unaware of the power of computer terminals in student hands.)

But the value of media as conduits of authentic information can be relative. In the face of Chinese government censorship of mainstream media, the Internet was the most reliable source. Yet, since the very beginnings of commercial online services in the early 1980s, the authenticity of e-mail and postings on online "bulletin boards" (1980s' parlance for what is in part encompassed today in Web logs) has been one its Achilles' heels.

If we already know the author of an e-mail, or the person with whom we are exchanging instant messages, we are likely to recognize an impersonation. But how can we have such confidence in a Web log written by someone we do not know? The blog from Baghdad could be written by a kid out for fun in Brooklyn. Worse, it could be written by a propagandist at the Pentagon or any other country. Aliases and spoofs are alas as fundamental a component of publishing on the Internet as its freedom from editorial—and, for the most part, govern- mental—regulation. (The U.S. Supreme Court decision in June 2003 to allow withdrawal of federal funding to libraries that do not take steps to block the access of children to online pornography is a very minor step toward increased federal supervision. Unlike the Communications Decency Act of 1996, rightly set aside by the Supreme Court as violating the First Amendment to the Constitution, the library ruling does not directly muzzle the Internet.)

The cellphone, even without the videophone, has no such impersonation problem. The voice that speaks words is obvi- ously recognizable in a way that the fingers that type words are not. Indeed, digital technology has undermined the ancient authenticity of writing. In a handwritten age, a reader could at least recognize the penmanship of the writer. Even the type-writer provided a degree of uniqueness, if not in the hand that typed, at least in the machine, and whether the tops of the t's or bottoms of the y's were bent, broken, or otherwise unusual. But nowadays the words that appear on our computer screen are the result of impersonal binary code, which in turn is the result of letters that are pressed on a keyboard. The kind of keyboard, the length and speed of the fingers, the size of the hand, bear no connection whatsoever to what the letters look like on the reader's screen. All that the hand and the brain that directs its amanuensis determine is what the letters are. It is almost as if the mind is writing directly, summoning letters that are immaculate or at any rate untouched by physical properties of fingers and hands. The chain between author and words is so spare that the only way a reader can know who a writer is with any confidence is if the writer is already known to the reader, and the writer's personality and writing style—the writer's mind, and what and how the writer writes—is therefore identifiable.

In contrast, the cellphone, for all its high-tech operation, works in the most fundamental realm of human communica-tion: the voice. Even a baby who knows no language can recognize its mother's voice. For years studies have suggested that babies may even respond to voices heard in the womb.

Cellphonic reporting thus is intrinsically more reliable, at least regarding source, than any text on the Web. This does not mean the cellphone cannot be used by a journalist to deceive. Indeed, Jayson Blair, as mentioned above, used the cellphone to lie about his whereabouts to the *New York Times*. But once Blair's deception was uncovered, the very same cellphone made it impossible for him to deny that it was he who placed the deceptive calls. The cellphone had conveyed his uniquely recognizable voice.

The Internet's inability to provide such basic authenticity is likely one of the reasons that it failed to play a more primary role in reporting the Iraqi War. Surveys conducted during and after the war showed that twenty-four-hour, all-news cable television made the largest gains in audience, or, in Internet terms, numbers of users. Fox News led the surge, with a 300 percent growth to 3.3 million viewers per day. The traditional broadcast networks in the United States—ABC, CBS, and NBC—actually lost 10 percent of their viewers, but still managed to attract an average of 28 million a day, compared to the 7 to 8 million daily viewers of cable. All of this television was powered by the cellphone. As Andrew Hayward, president of CBS News noted, "This was a reporter's war, not an anchor's war," because the reporters were embedded and able to convey firsthand, immediate information—words, sounds, and images—via cellphones. (See Steve Schifferes, "Who Won the US Media War," 2003, for additional details.)

The weakness of the Internet blogs was that most of the writers were correctly perceived as something less than professional reporters. And for all of its immediacy, the Internet also lacked the advantage of all television and radio—even pre-cable, pre-cellphonic TV—of being available at the press of a button or turn of a switch. The Web needs to be logged on to (and the awkwardness of that phrase is apt, because it conveys the uncomfortable amount of time that can intervene between sitting down at or with a computer and reading a Web page).

In the end, then, the Internet as a vehicle of war reportage was impressive mostly in comparison to the traditional newspaper, which, despite the apparent authenticity of its journalism—the Jayson Blair fiasco notwithstanding—was nonetheless hopelessly yesterday's news, literally and figuratively, and thus no match for the instant coverage of all electronic media, even including the log-on lag time of the Internet. The time lapse of the newspaper also made it unfit to capitalize on the embedded cellphonic journalist, and thus the printed press was all the more trounced by TV and its cellphones. The Internet could and did offer embedded cell-phonic reports, but these were less clear and convenient than the same reports provided on television. The Internet thus was left to make its stand on the potential quicksand of the blog. The result was less than might have been predicted in the golden dawn of the Web just a decade ago, prior to the marriage of cellphones and TV journalism.

Cellphones as Weapons of War: The Cellphonic Fuse

The same characteristics that make the cellphone an ideal instrument of war reporting—live connections to reporters on the scene, wherever they happened to be—make it an ideal instrument for war, or military communication. New communication technologies often have served important, pivotal roles in war. Lincoln not only authorized Brady's battlefield photography, but kept in close contact with Grant via telegraph in the closing days of the Civil War. (Ironically, the first reports of Lincoln's assassination to reach Reuter's in London—via telegram from a reporter in Ireland, who had just crossed the Atlantic—were not believed, in part because the telegraph was less trusted than face-to-face communication or handwritten correspondence. The telegraph, likely because it was the very first electronic medium, had a long acceptance curve: Congress took five years to decide to allocate funding for telegraph lines in America, after Morse's demonstration to President Van Buren in 1838 convinced him of its merits, and Van Buren asked Congress for support.) Franklin Delano Roosevelt and all of the major political leaders in World War II, as we have seen, used radio to inspire and marshal their people. Roosevelt also—like Lyndon Johnson two decades later—liked to work the telephone. (Roosevelt even had his phone number listed in the 1931 New York City phone book when he was governor of New York.) In contrast, his successor, Harry Truman, disliked the phone. According to his biographer David McCullough (1992, pp. 141–42), Truman was a "nineteenth-century man," who, in addition to the telephone, had little use for typewriters, Duchamp's "Nude Descending a Staircase," and jazz. But John F. Kennedy thought enough of the phone that he installed the "hot line" between New York and Moscow after the Cuban Missile Crisis, as a way of allowing him and Soviet Premier Nikita Khrushchev to keep in direct contact and prevent wars. Both men realized that the crisis had been fed in part by lack of information, and misunderstanding of the other leader's intentions. Unfortunately, neither survived much longer in office to make use of this phone connection.

In actual military operations, radio walkie-talkies have been in common use since World War II, and the Navy made use of wireless in World War I. (The U.S. Navy thought wireless telegraphy—early radio—so essential that it sought, unsuccessfully, to make radio a government monopoly.) Cellphone technology improved and streamlined the walkie-talkie. But cellphones also played another military role in the Iraqi War, a special assignment that only the cellphone and its widespread non-military use around the world could have undertaken. After the two direct missile attacks on Saddam Hussein, or places where the Iraqi leader was presumed to be—the first at the start of the war, the second a few weeks later—questions arose in the media about how the coalition could have had such explicit information about Saddam's whereabouts. Not surprisingly, no definitive answer was provided. But "background" sources indicated that the United States had been in touch with Iraqis close to Saddam Hussein, just prior to the missile attacks, via e-mail and cellphone.

Unless the Iraqi informants carried sophisticated Palm Pilots that allowed reliable, verifiable e-mail with U.S. agents—and, as we have just seen above, no e-mail is that reliable—the most likely medium at use in these circumstances would have been the cellphone. We can envision the following scenario: Someone in Saddam Hussein's presence, or near enough to know exactly where he was, excuses him- or herself, ducks into a bathroom or other suitable private place, and makes a cellphone call. This person presumably has previously been in touch with a coalition contact. The cellphone call provides exact details on Saddam's location—both in the verbal description given by the caller and perhaps in electronic satellite triangulation on the source of the call. The cellphone has just become, from Saddam's perspective, the enemy's invisible ears. But the ears do more than hear; they pack an awesome punch. The information they convey triggers a ferocious missile attack a few minutes later. (Whether the attack succeeds depends on factors other than the cellphone: is the information reliable, is the informant a double agent, is Saddam still in the restaurant, etc? In these two instances, we know that it did not. In any case, given the power and speed of the missile attack, the informant had better leave not only the table but the premises, completely and quickly.)

When we consider the fact that secretly planted bombs have long been deployed in attempts to destroy enemy leaders in war, we can appreciate the difference made by the cellphonic fuse. The bomb plot against Adolf Hitler in 1944, brought off by dissident German military leaders, succeeded in setting off a bomb, if not right in Hitler's face, under the very table where he sat. But he was wounded, not killed, and his address to the German people that night on radio convinced the rest of the military leadership that he was not seriously hurt. As a result, they stayed loyal to, if discontented with, the Third Reich; the insurrection was stopped, and the war continued. A bigger bomb under the table might have killed Hitler and ended the war right then. But there was no way such a weapon could have been smuggled into the room and hidden.

The cellphone, in contrast, allows deployment of thousands of bombs on a target of assassination, each more than a thousand times as powerful as the bomb that wounded Hitler. Connected to the massive, immediately deployable missile might of a country such as the United States, a single cellphone becomes an unprecedented weapon of pinpoint accuracy and enormous power. The instrument of social disruption, in receipt of calls in restaurants, theaters, and funeral homes, becomes an instrument of political and physical disruption, of palpable, bloody destruction, in the theater of war. Indeed, a restaurant would have been the scene of this disruption in the Iraqi War, if it had been true that Saddam Hussein was dining in the restaurant that was the target of the second missile attack that was called in on him—likely, *literally* called in—in April of 2003.

Thus, from the standpoint of Saddam's regime, the cellphone apparently became a two-edged sword that cut against its throat, an instrument of communication that became an instrument of intrusion—just as in the hands of anyone who, for whatever reason, would rather not receive a call at a given time. Except that, in the case of the former Iraqi regime, the intrusion was lethal—that is, lethal to Saddam's government, not the man.

What would prevent our enemies from using the cellphone in the same way against us? Surely there are at least a few spies with cellphones in our midst.

Nothing would prevent this—other than the fact that our enemies, at present, do not have the kind of quickly launchable, precisely guided, overwhelming missile power that we possess. We thus benefited, in the Iraqi War, from a profound asymmetry in communications and weaponry around the world: Everyone around the world has cellphones; only the coalition had the decisive missile follow-through. Or, stated otherwise, because only we had the missiles, we benefited from cellphones in Baghdad but Saddam Hussein did not benefit from cellphones in Washington, London, Sydney, Madrid, and other coalition capitals.

So, absent immediately deployable missiles, the cellphone is deprived of its best punch as a piece of war machinery. But this does not mean that the ubiquitous cellphone is or will be a toothless tiger as a weapon for everyone except the United

States and its allies. The FBI's investigation of the May 2003 terrorist bombing in Riyadh, Saudi Arabia (which killed thirty-five people), found modified cellphones that could set off a bomb with a call. (See Anderson, 2003, for details.) Presumably al-Qaeda and the September 11 terrorists used cellphones in their planning. Indeed, the role of new media— meaning, cellphones and the Internet—in terrorist operations, from September 11 on down, is still one of the unreported, perhaps unknown components in that as-yet mostly unexplained catastrophe. If the full story of how September 11 happened ever comes out—how the FBI and American law enforcement were caught so off-guard—it may well tell us that too much attention was accorded to old media, such as taps for landline telephones, and not enough to new media such as cellphones and the anonymous Internet. (We do know and commemorate, of course, the crucial use of cellphones by Todd Beamer, Jeremy Glick, and others on the hijacked United Airlines Flight 93, and their prevention of that plane from doing far more damage.) As for missiles that can take out restaurants anyplace in the world on just a few minutes' notice at the call of a cellphone—these are bound to proliferate and get into lots of arsenals, as has just about every other weapon in history. Japanese rejection of the gun as a dishonorable weapon for more than three hundred years is perhaps the best, but still ultimately unsuccessful, exception. (See Noel Perrin's 1979 *Giving Up the Gun: Japan's Reversion to the Sword, 1543–1879*, for the fascinating account.)

So the cellphone, like any other possible weapons system— like any other technology, period—can be used for good or bad. There is no such thing as an intrinsically, inevitably always-good or always-bad technology. I have been delivering a lecture on and off for three decades at conferences on technology and ethics that I think brings home this point. I call it "Guns, Knives, and Pillows." (I've written about it, too, briefly. See, for example, my "On Behalf of Humanity: The Technological Edge," 1996.) Can we think of an inherently bad technology, one that we and the world would have been better off had the technology not been invented? The gun is an obvious choice. But in addition to the rejoinder of a gun in the hands of someone trying to stop a murder (a just war would be a special case of this), a gun also can be used to hunt an animal and prevent starvation. In this circumstance, the gun is clearly not being used for evil, or, at least, not for anything that is on balance evil, unless we were to hold that killing an animal was worse than allowing a human being to starve to death. Okay, but what about an intrinsically good technology, which is at worst inobtrusive and never does anyone any harm? How about a pillow? All it seems to do, quietly, is make our head or other part of our body more comfortable. But, alas, it also can be used to murder someone via suffocation.

Perhaps our problem in this reckoning is that we did not go far enough and were too tame in our choices of seemingly evil and good technologies. Let's say we substituted the atom bomb for the gun? Nuclear weapons can and have wreaked far more destruction than any gun. And even when used for peaceful, good purposes—such as producing energy—the nuclear option can lead to great harm, as in the meltdown at Chernobyl. But every malignant tumor that has ever been shrunk, slowed, or destroyed by medical radiation provides an exception to the equation of splitting the atom and evil, and should give pause to the thought that our species would have been better off had twentieth-century physics never existed. In other words, medicine, and thus radiation used for medicine, is good. But . . . is medicine always good? Have we at last identified in the technology of cure, ranging from radiation to vaccines, something far more undilutedly good than the humble pillow? No, not at all. For germ warfare, bred from the same medical technology as vaccines, is as bad as nuclear weapons, maybe even worse, in its capacity to wipe out three-fifths of the world's population, as happened in some parts of Europe from the natural disaster of the Black Plague. Indeed, bio-weapons were right up there along with nuclear weapons (and chemical weapons) in the weapons of mass destruction the United States was looking to eradicate in Saddam Hussein's Iraq. The relatively low expense of bio-weapons, the devastating way in which deadly germs, once set loose, can spread themselves, has given them the label of the poor-man's atom bomb.

It thus seems that, no matter how hard and far we press our case—no matter how exhaustive and extreme we are in our attempt to identify unambiguously, unalterably bad or good technology—we arrive at the realization that all technologies, even the seeming bad and good, are like knives, which can be used to cut people (bad) or food (good). And the cellphone is in many ways the epitome of this two-edged sword of technology. As a communications medium, it immensely increases our access to others (whether they like it or not) while increasing their access to us (whether we like it or not). As a medium in war, it provides unprecedented access to the process, and sometimes becomes part of the process itself—which, in war, means it not only communicates but can kill, and can prevent killing.

Microcosm and Future

Wars always have been microcosms of the future, crucibles of time in which technologies just on the verge of coming true give us a preview, strut their stuff under the incredible pressure of life and death, the need to win, to survive. The semaphore came of age in the Napoleonic wars and pointed the way to the telegraph. The space age and the nuclear age both debuted in World War II, with the German V2 rocket and the American atom bomb. So, too, did the cellphone—or, at very least, a technology of talking long distance on the run, the walkie-talkie.

The future of more than one technology of communication became clear in the handful of intense weeks of the Iraqi War.

The videophone, hooked up to the cellphone, in turn hooked up to television, truly entered the mainstream for the first time. All-news cable television, which entered the fray for the first time via CNN in the first Gulf War, became the undeniable first-rung medium of war coverage in the second Gulf War, even if ratings for cable stations still were behind those of the traditional broadcast networks. The number of cable viewers during the war grew enormously, while the number of network viewers, with the partial exception of NBC, shrank. The future of news on television seems pretty clear.

CBS-TV decided on the first weekend of the war to interrupt its twenty-four-hour coverage with a college basketball game, in pursuit of higher ratings. And differences in the numbers of cable and broadcast viewers reflect more than simply the preferences of all possible TV viewers. Cable service, after all, still costs money, and the total number of people with cable in the United States is still less than the total number of people with television—some 80 percent, in contrast to the 99 percent of American households with TV. So, in competing for viewers of war coverage, cable was fighting with one hand, or at least a finger or two on that hand, tied behind its back. The handwriting is still written on the screen. (The only time— as of December 2003—a cable program attracted more viewers than any network broadcast was for the September 2002 premier of the fourth season of *The Sopranos* on HBO. During the Iraqi War, Fox News was often the most-watched station on all of cable, an accomplishment of all-news cable attained only once before, by CNN in 1991 during the first Gulf War.)

The Internet did all right, too, and war blogs attracted a lot of notice, but the future of the Web revealed in the Iraqi War was more narrow, less predominant than many predicted in the last decade. Other than the blogs, the Web played a cooperative, even subsidiary role to older media such as television in coverage of the war, rather than vice versa. This smaller role for the Internet as a news medium was consistent with Web expectations deflated in many other areas in the past few years, including online shopping. Amazon, for example, still accounts for only 8 percent of retail book sales in the United States. (The overwhelming rest of books are purchased at in-person bookstores such as Barnes & Noble, Borders, and independent bookshops.) Pornography, not easily available in person, and music, either available for free but fleetingly on radio, or very expensively in stores, continue to move briskly on the Web.

Traditional newspapers, inevitably a day behind, slid further into a future of dwindling impact. This was no surprise, and has been under way since first radio and then television began stealing the thunder of the printed press.

Behind a lot of this revolution was the cellphone/videophone combination. Available any time night or day, anytime an embedded journalist was able to get through with a call, the cellphone catered not to the traditional network newscast, which even in expanded form was on just a few hours every day; not to the Internet, which had to be logged on to, and with a lack of clarity of image that exacerbated the grainy videophone; and certainly not the printed, hobbling newspaper. Instead, the cellphone worked perfectly with the 24/7 all-news cable station.

But what lessons can we learn from this about the cellphone not at war, in the years ahead, other than that it will have a continuing role in news and, in that role, at least, a continuing relationship with the videophone?

The cellphone has become so light, so small, so easy to put in a pocket, that only a naked person has an excuse not to have one on his or her person.

In the next and final chapter, we explore the future of the cellphone and, in particular, what we can do to direct its two-edged sword not only to the good, but to the best it can do for us in all walks of life.

Chapter 11
Future Calls

The unintended consequences of new technology do not mean that we cannot plan and refine and improve our technologies and the way they operate. Although our plans may not turn out just as we expected, half a loaf of satisfaction with an improved device is still better than none.

The cellphone, as we have seen, has had more than its share of unforeseen drawbacks. Among the most irritating of these is the irony that the more we use cellphones—the more they do for us, the better they work—the more we resent the times they do not. When a device is very new, any service we get from it can seem miraculous. When we become accustomed to it, we take its service for granted, and any loss or lack of service ranges from annoying to intolerable.

Our response to speed is an excellent example of our insatiable appetite for perfect communication—"perfect" being communication in complete accordance with what our imaginations and impulses dangle in front of us. In the early days of telecommunicating personal computers, in the first half of the 1980s, modems that transmitted data at 300 and then 1,200 bits per second seemed lightning fast. And they were, in comparison to their predecessors, which worked at one-third or one-twelfth the speed. Today a modem that connects to the Web at 56,000 bits per second can feel painfully slow, arthritic. And in fact it is, for many services—such as streaming video—on the Web. But even the fastest ISDN or cable-modem connection can frustrate, if it conveys information to us even a drop slower than the absolute immediacy of our imagination.

Indeed, it is the very speed of electronic communication—186,000 miles per second, the speed of light, the fastest speed in the universe, according to Einstein—that frustrates us, when it does not equal the even faster effective speed of imagination. This problem usually does not arise in transportation. We can be leaning on a lamppost on Forty-second Street in New York City and imagine ourselves talking to someone similarly inclined on Piccadilly Circus in London. If we wish to make the trip physically, we understand that travel to Kennedy Airport, across the Atlantic Ocean by air, and then from Heathrow Airport to the heart of London is going to take some time. (Alas, more now than it used to, due to the Concorde's untimely passing in 2003.) But if we wish to speak to someone in London by cellphone, and circuits are busy, or we get chopped off in midsentence, we find those kinds of delays evidence of the poor quality of the cellphone system and really unacceptable.

So the cellphone can be the victim of its own success, a target of ire due to the expectations it raises. But the cellphone also has the big disadvantage—almost just the reverse, discussed earlier in this book—of making us accessible when we may want to be unreachable, private, alone. Yes, we can pretend we were in a silent pocket, or our cellphone in our pocket was off, but do we really want the age of the cellphone also to be the heroic age of the little white lie?

In this chapter we consider how these and other shortcomings and unwanted effects of the cellphone can be removed or reduced in ways that do not introduce too many new, unexpected problems. Of course, to the extent that such problems are truly unintended and unforeseen, we are not likely to know much about them, no matter how hard we try to fathom and chart them beforehand, anyway. So we still wind up proceeding somewhat blindly. But three blind mice—or, at least, three myopic rodents—are the inevitable way of technological planning and progress. We can help by implanting at least the partially corrective lenses of what has happened before with other technologies and their unintended consequences, and what has happened thus far with the cellphone. And the good news is that even when our remedies for existing problems create new problems, we are free to devise remedies (albeit imperfect) for these new problems, too.

So the imprecise, give-and-take process of media evolution continues. And if, at any given time, we can say that a technology and the remedies we have devised for its drawbacks provide us with more benefits than we had before, if we can say that the mixture of old and new services and pros and cons of a device helps us, on balance, more than a previous device with its admixture of services and pluses and minuses—if they give more than they take—then we can rightly say that we have made progress.

Tailoring the Telephone

The cellphone itself, just as it is today, is a masterful remedy for perhaps the most profound drawback of the phone attached by wire or screw to a wall: missing a crucial call, or not being able to make a crucial call at the moment you need to make it. Indeed, the landline telephone probably has been subject to more significant improvements than any other medium since its invention in 1876; it is a veritable textbook for the operation of remedial media.

A mere year after the telephone's invention by Bell, Edison thought that his just-invented phonograph would be a telephone answering machine. That this vision took nearly a hundred years to implement does not change the fact that, almost from the moment of its inception, the telephone was considered a prime target for improvement. The miracle of talking to someone not physically present was so profound and unprecedented that people wanted to perfect it. Like speed in communication, the first taste of it summoned an appetite for more and better.

The telephone answering machine was a nearly flawless improvement. While it by no means remedied all problems of missed calls—some people prefer not to leave messages (perhaps they do not want to surrender the initiation of the call to the person being called, and want to keep the element of surprise)—it introduced very few new ones. From the perspective of the person who installs a telephone answering machine (or uses voice mail, the current name for this—an interesting back-formation from e-mail), the one disadvantage is the loss of plausible deniability that you missed a call from someone you do not want to speak to on the phone. In the good old days, you could have no idea who called you at home when you were out of the house. You could even let your phone ring, unanswered, when you were home, if you suspected the caller was a bill collector, an in-law, or someone else you wished to avoid. Nowadays, with the missed call recorded, your only recourse is to claim the machine or the voice mail was not working properly (another thread in the tapestry of white lies we often need to weave around ourselves in the new information age). But this drawback seems minor compared to the obvious advantage of getting messages from people you do want to hear from when you're away from your phone. And the cellphone in turn improves on this by sharply limiting the time you are away from your phone. Indeed, the cellphone pretty much reduces that time to sojourns in deep sleep and the shower (and, as far as sleep goes, the cellphone gives new meaning to the expression "sound asleep"—you're sound asleep if you're asleep to the sound of the phone, which is less often than years ago, since a cellphone can awaken you from a nap in the hammock, away from the landline phone near your bed).

The blessings of call waiting, call forwarding, and caller ID, introduced in limited areas in the early 1970s (one was the Grand Concourse/Fordham Road area of the Bronx, where I lived at that time), and pretty much commonplace by the mid-1990s, are more mixed. Call forwarding, increasingly unnecessary in the age of the cellphone, is the least problematic. Your calls are forwarded from home or other phone to whatever phone you specify. The only drawback is the same as the answering machine's: call forwarding may bring a call to your ear that you prefer not to receive.

The advantages and disadvantages of call waiting are a little more complex. Before call waiting, one could miss a call not only by being away from the phone, but by being on the phone, talking to someone else. From the caller's point of view, a busy signal at least provided more information than an unanswered ring, because the busy signal told the caller that someone—if not necessarily the person being called—was at home, using the phone. Business offices usually did not have this problem. Receptionists who answered the phone would explain that the party being called was on another call, not in the office, not otherwise available, whatever. More recently, even smaller businesses had multiple phone lines, which bounced an incoming call on a number in use to an open line, which visibly flashed to the person on the phone. (Nowadays, much of this shuttling consists of automatic bouncing to voice mail.) But the busy signal at home or the receptionist at work nonetheless could defeat the caller's need to talk to someone immediately, and this could generate an irritation all its own. Call waiting solves most of this problem: the caller hears a ring, not a busy signal, and the person already talking on the phone hears a beep and has the option of putting the first person on hold and attending to the new caller. The person already talking thus takes on the powers of the receptionist, or, looked at technically, now has a multiple system on a single-line phone. In either rendition, the person who has call waiting has more options and control.

But this control also creates a new series of dilemmas, perhaps as aggravating as the problems that call waiting solves. If you are talking on the phone and another call comes in, and you put the first person on hold, then return a few seconds later and say you have to conclude the conversation, what message are you giving to the first person on the phone: that his or her conversation was just chopped liver, not as important to you as the second call? You could, of course, just ignore the new incoming call, but then you would be missing or delaying that conversation, and on that score you would be no better off than you were before call waiting was invented. (Caller ID could at least tell you whom the new call was from. But deliberate non-use of a new technology, or inability to use it, still can be discomforting, as when the family acquires a new automobile and you're stuck driving the old heap. You can be better off, in some of those cases, if the new technology had not been available in the first place.) All in all, call waiting is certainly advantageous in emergencies (though, prior to call waiting, operators could be asked to break into conversations for personal or business emergencies). It is also good to have in less urgent situations, when you are concluding your initial conversation, and/or the new person calling is someone you really want to hear from. But the potential for unintended insult means you need to proceed carefully. (Intended insult is no problem, if you're sure the object is deserving.) In assuming the powers of the receptionist, the person wielding call waiting is deprived of the traditional cover of the rude, inept receptionist being the reason the important call did not get through.

Caller ID is at once the most helpful and troublesome of all of these telephonic remedies. The capacity to identify your caller, before you accept the call, means you can easily avoid the unwanted phone call. Telephone rings can be ignored safely, whether on primary or forwarded phones. The magical, compelling, boundless ambiguity of the telephone's ring—the call could be from anyone, the love of your life, your business partner on the deal of your life, the agent, editor, producer who will make you famous, in other words, the person you most want to hear from—is brought within less demanding bounds: you can see who is calling you before you pick up the phone. Of course, until you look at the caller ID read out—if you hear the phone ring in another room—you still are subject to its irresistible pull. But this is the least of the limitations of caller ID.

One of the great—great as in good, or beneficial—
unintended consequences of the original telephone was
precisely that the caller was unknown, until he or she spoke.
No other form of interpersonal communication allowed such
anonymity. People do not regularly initiate conversations in
person with bags over their heads, and letters arrive in
envelopes that usually have the sender's name in plain sight.
E-mail and instant messaging, as discussed in the previous chapter, allow anonymity throughout the entire communication—
not just at the outset—and, for that matter, allow outright
deception in identity. But the initial anonymity of the phone
caller, during the ring, before the voice is heard, was in many
ways more profound, because it was a natural, intrinsic aspect
of the telephone system, rather than a deliberate choice, as in
e-mail, when the sender chooses a screen name meant to
conceal or deceive.

In what ways was this initial, unavoidable masking of the
telephone caller an advantage? Well, it was certainly not a plus
for the recipient of an obscene or otherwise harassing phone
call, and this was and is rightly cited as a general societal benefit of caller ID. (The direct mouth-to-ear connection on the
phone, with no intervening parties, facilitates obscene calls,
just as it works well for phone sex. Obscene telegrams were
never much of a problem.) But what about all other callers?
The element of surprise, lost when one leaves a voice mail message, becomes lost to all callers all the time when all phones
are outfitted with caller ID. Most of the time, this does not
matter. But what about in business dealings, in which you do
not want your interest in having a conversation known until
the instant that you actually start the conversation? What
about when you're calling someone up to ask them out, and
you're not sure how your call will be received, and you'd prefer the matter be decided on the dulcet persuasions of your
voice, rather than the party not even hearing your story
because she or he did not want to speak to you then? The
course of true love never did run smooth, including through

phone lines, but caller ID has no doubt on occasion tangled them even further.

The telephone, of course, was not deliberately designed to give callers the advantage of initial anonymity. But in a world in which the default for all other communication was not anonymous, the telephone's anonymity could be a useful, even welcome, departure from the norm. There was an almost self-effacing, Victorian modesty about this aspect of phone life, which spanned most of the twentieth century. You were simply anonymous in making a call, before it was answered, without making a public statement that you wanted to be anonymous. You were initially a cipher in your approach on the phone because that was the only way a phone call could be made. The phone cipher was thus innocent (with the exception of the obscene caller, who took advantage of this characteristic), in contrast to today's cyber cypher—the spoofer, the pretender, the role-player—who traffics at the height of deliberate deceit and calculation.

Caller ID robbed the phone caller of that innocent veil. Predictably, that evoked a response: a method of masking the caller's identity, for caller ID–enabled phones. And this predictably evoked a counterresponse: blocking of calls in which the identity of the caller was masked. Was this cascade of measures and countermeasures and the net loss of modesty all worth the checkmate of the obscene caller? Perhaps living in a more attributable society is better. Or maybe the capacity to take a first tentative step, via untraceable phone call, is an opportunity we'll miss. Likely we'll never know for sure. Subtle changes such as this are very difficult to track.

The Eyes Don't Yet Have It

Sometimes a remedial technology creates so many potential new problems—or seems that it will create them—that it never gets off the ground in the first place. The videophone—a telephone that allows the talkers to be seen as well as heard—has been described as the next logical step for the telephone for almost as long as the answering machine. Tom Swift used one in his fictional adventures as early as 1914 (*Tom Swift and His Photo Telephone*). Some of the early experiments that led to television actually were videophone, as when then Secretary of Commerce Herbert Hoover talked to AT&T's president Walter S. Gifford in a "wire television" conversation between Washington, D.C., and New York in 1927. Harry Granick's classic 1947/1991 *Underneath New York* (p. 146) notes that "Bell engineers are surely developing the most amazing stage of distance communication, the stage wherein we will not only speak with distant friends but see them"; alas, the historical descriptions in Granick's book were superior to its predictions. Successive World's Fairs touted Bell Telephone's "Picturephone." But Brenda Maddox, writing in *Beyond Babel* (p. 207) in 1972, was still right to observe that "if a single piece of new communication technology has been advertised in advance, it is the picture telephone, yet there is little sign of any demand for it."

Eventually the Internet, the medium of media, got into the picture. By the end of the 1990s, "C-U See Me" and similar Web programs allowed conversations with voices and images. But these, like many other Web tricks, never made the jump from cool gimmick to replacement of traditional, off-line, older medium, in this case, the telephone. (On the other hand, it is worth noting that mainstream media often make their first appearance in the popular culture as toys, to amuse and amaze, rather than to communicate. Edison's first motion pictures were just minutes long, and were enjoyed for the thrill of seeing motion captured, rather than the tiny story they told. The telephone itself, as we saw in Chapter 1, was dismissed by the head of Western Union Telegraph as a "toy," and similar convictions in England slowed its adoption there for decades.

See my "Toy, Mirror, and Art: The Metamorphosis of Technological Culture," 1977, for more details, including what circumstances may be necessary for maturation from the toy stage. The point about the videophone is that it has been arrested in the juvenile toy stage for most of its existence.)

War, as discussed in the prior chapter, can be a cauldron for the emergence and refinement of new media. In the Iraqi War, the video-cellphone and its connection to television provided extraordinary, unprecedented, firsthand, immediate coverage, by enabling embedded and other reporters to sometimes show us events in the field as they were happening. In the aftermath of September 11, 2001, videoconferencing became an attractive alternative to flying across the country for business meetings. Perhaps coincidentally, perhaps because of this new (or renewed) emphasis on pictures and phones, a new feature was promoted for the cellphone in 2003: a digital camera built right into the phone, which could snap instant color photographs and send them to someone's e-mail address or cellphone. Some models could even shoot and transmit video clips. (See, for example, Rothman's "Gadget of the Week," 2003.) But even these photos and clips were forms of personal reporting rather than live video conversation—send a new snapshot of the baby to Grandma, or (a frequent subject of the advertisements for these "camera" phones on television) nab a friend making a buffoon of himself, and send it out to all and sundry. (And the camera phones have the troublesome unintended consequence of allowing photos to be taken surreptitiously, in crowded trains, up women's skirts; see Kageyama, "Camera-Equipped Phones Spread Mischief," 2003.)

Thus, as a vehicle of simple talk between everyday people, rather than a means of reporting or high-powered, specially arranged meetings for business, the videophone still remains at the beginning of the twenty-first century the aging heir apparent of the telephone. (I first gave the videophone that label in "Human Replay," back in 1979.) Whether by landline or cell, most folks apparently have no keen need to see the people they are talking to on the phone or (likely more to the point) to be seen.

Why is this so? Television, after all, did replace radio as the after-dinner, evening, living-room medium. We have eyes as well as ears—in real life we usually see as well as hear the people we're talking to, as well as most events we witness, so the advent of television makes perfect sense. It's only natural that we design media to accomplish across great distances of space and time what we do, close at hand, as we walk through the world. Indeed, radio no doubt survived only because there are times in the natural world, crucial times, when we hear without seeing anything (as when a sound awakens us in the morning) or when we hear something emanating from a source quite different from what we are looking at (as when we hear a cry of help or alarm from behind, or over the hill). (I call this movement of media toward more natural forms, and the survival of media that achieve some naturally human ecological niche—which is the case for both television and radio—the "anthropotropic" evolution of media, as in "anthropo" meaning human and "tropic" meaning toward. In terms of Darwinian natural selection, we might say that *we* are the "natural" environment that selects media for survival, based on how well they extend our communication without disrupting our biological expectations. I developed this theory in my doctoral dissertation, "Human Replay: A Theory of the Evolution of Media," in the late 1970s.) So radio flourishes in kitchens, bathrooms, and cars, where hearing something unrelated to your eating, bathing, or driving works well. Television is a benefit only to the passenger of the car, not the driver who cannot afford to be visually distracted, and cellphones with images would be as dangerous to the driver as television—even more so, since the driver would be looking at a person on the screen who was talking directly to him or her. This is why even the entirely acoustic, nonvisual traditional cellphone, unlike one-way radio, which does not entail conversation, must be used carefully by drivers. (I think we are just getting to the point where we can call the first mass-market cellphones of the 1990s "traditional.") But why have we not seen the spread of videophones in homes, offices, and streets, indeed, in any hands not on the steering wheel, in daily life?

Economics no doubt stopped the videophone at first. As we saw in Chapter 9, machines that receive audiovisual signals were a lot less expensive than technologies of production and transmission. Thus one-way television, which receives but cannot transmit, was the outgrowth of Hoover's "wire television" conversation, not the videophone.

But there were reasons deeper than economics, more impressive than money (with all due respect to Karl Marx), for the videophone's lack of public reception. People enjoyed the unintended invisibility of the original telephone. They took advantage—we still take advantage—of the opportunity to talk to someone regardless of what we are wearing (or not wearing). In general, we do like to see whom we are talking to—we would just as soon see, if not necessarily what you are wearing, certainly the expression on your face. This was and is the impetus for the videophone. But we may or may not want the person with whom we are conversing to see us, if, unlike in the natural world of conversation, we have any control over this. (For years I have asked students in my undergraduate classes if they would accept a gift of a videophone, on the condition only that they would have to use it. Most say no. The reason most given for declining my hypothetical offer is that the would-be recipients didn't want to have to think about what they look like when they talk on the phone. Among the few who have said yes, one young woman offered that a videophone would allow her to show off her new outfits to her friends and seek their advice about what to wear. In other words, this positive response was the flip side of the negative: both hinged on the pros and cons of being seen, rather than the advantage of seeing others.) (Web cams, pornographic and otherwise, are another interesting example,

relatively rare in the overall population: the installer of the
Web cam *wants* to be seen.)

The mixture of public and private in the home since the
phone—the public colonization of the private home via the
conquistador of the phone—had some adverse effects, notably
the loss of inaccessibility in the home, when we want to be
beyond public reach. But the mixture also had the advantage
of allowing us to dress privately, any way we pleased, and talk
publicly from the home—a benefit the videophone would
eliminate. This points to another reason (in addition to dis-
comfort with flying) that videoconferencing has caught on, at
least a bit, for business meetings: anyone at and on the job is
likely already dressed, if not for success, certainly for business.
Presumably people out of the house, in the street or in a car,
are also more publicly dressed than folks at home. This fact of
life suggests that the videophone may indeed have better luck
in cellphones, outside of the home, than in phones, landline or
cellphone, in the home. (But the driver of a car, as indicated,
has very good reason not to want a videophone, whatever his
or her sartorial mien.)

Should the videophone ever replace the home audiophone
("audiophone," a reasonable retro-formation to the degree that
videophone has any chance of taking over at home, or on the
street), we of course will be able to devise remedial features to
counter the loss of privacy caused by the gain of face. Remedies
for remedies, the way of evolution. We could have a "modesty
screen," which would be displayed to callers whenever we did
not wish to be seen. These, in turn, would not be perfect solu-
tions, in this case because their use would be making a specific
statement that we did not want to be seen. (Parents would likely
assume the worst of their children: they don't want to be seen
because they have something to hide in their physical appearance. This was also a reason given by my undergraduate students
for not wanting a videophone.) As with love and the telephone,
the course of true remedial media never did run smooth.

Wish List for the Cellphone

If the history of the telephone is any lesson, we should be careful what we wish for regarding the cellphone. Nonetheless, in the sea of unintended consequences, several improvements seem relatively clear sailing.

Here I offer but one for the caller, and one for the called. The cellphone and its impact can be seen as a cat-and-mouse game between caller and called, in which each jockeys for advantage, each seeks to maximize the benefits of being in touch, without losing privacy, inaccessibility, or one of the desired characteristics of the pre-cellphone age.

It thus seems fair to provide an improvement to the caller, which will make the called more accessible, and an improvement for the called, which will make the called less accessible, or give the called more control over receipt of calls. These improvements require no great leaps in technology, and thus could be implemented in the near future.

For the caller: A cellphone program that would allow the caller to store all known phone numbers for each name in the caller's directory, and rank them in order of most accessible, or most likely to result in the called receiving the call, live. Then, when the caller utters the name of the requested party, the cellphone automatically dials each stored number, in rank order, until a connection is made and a conversation takes place. There would be no limit on the quantity of phone numbers on the list, only that they all be legally obtained. The list could include all personal and business, landline and cell numbers for each individual, as well as those of the individual's spouse, family, friends, restaurants frequented, and so on—the good judgment of the caller, and the potential ire of the called, if an unacceptable phone number is called, would be the only practical restrictions. The result would magnify the cellphone's current great advantage to the caller: You can reach anyone you want to reach, anywhere you and they may be, any time you want to.

For the called: Different rings to identify different callers are already beginning to become available. But they do not go far enough. The easiest way of identifying a caller is to hear his or her voice. If you don't already know the caller's voice, you are no worse off than with an anonymous ring. If you do know the voice, you're much better off. Hearing the voice of your caller, before you accept the call, improves the benefit of caller ID: Sometimes there may be two or more people with access to the same phone, and you may want to speak to one but not the other. Seeing just a printout of the caller's number does not tell you who at that number is calling you. The voice does—it provides an indication of identity more reliable and authentic than any printed or written presentation. Only an image of the caller's face might be better—voices can be impersonated, faces cannot—but the possibilities in digital manipulation of images make any face that comes to us electronically as vulnerable to forgery as a voice. (In an age prior to Photoshop and its digital remaking of photographs, Tom Swift was able to say of his "photo telephone": "now persons using the wire can be sure of the other person they are conversing with"; Appleton, 1914, p. 126).

Hearing your caller's voice, instead of the ring, would require a bit more doing than the automated multiple dialer just described—in particular, it would require the caller to speak before placing the call, so the receiver would hear the caller's voice rather than the ring. In order to avoid faking— John uses Jim's phone to call Sarah, who accepts the call because she hears Jim's voice and wants to speak to him, not John—cellphones would have to be programmed to work only in response to a verbal command from a single voice, its owner's. This, of course, would create other problems, but that's inevitable with remedies.

Although the voice-ring benefits the called, not the caller, it thus would require the cooperation of the caller. But the person receiving the call also could program his or her cellphone to accept only calls that presented a voice, not a ring, and thereby encourage the caller to cooperate. (This would be similar to accepting only calls in which caller ID is not masked.)

The greater difficulty in improving the lot of the called rather than the caller brings home an enduring truth about cellphones: No matter how much we try to protect our wish and right to sometimes be inaccessible, the thrust of the cellphone, its bias, is toward extending the options and power of the caller. All media, as Harold Innis (1951) pointed out more than a half century ago, have certain "biases"—what we might today call spin—that continue to work, however we might try to direct them. Writing has a bias, a spin, toward permanence—toward lasting, enduring. We have to strive especially hard to devise erasers, physical and electronic, to remove what we have written. (This is why, decades after Innis died, computer programmers had to create "burn" commands, which not only erased data, but erased data in a way that made it utterly irretrievable. The key was in effect writing over the data when it was erased, rather than just removing its marker, which is the method of non-burning deletions and allows recovery of the data. See my "Nine Lives of Electronic Text," 1992, for more. Interestingly, we now also use the word "burn" in an opposite way, as in "burning" or recording data on CDs.) Speech has a bias toward dissemination. Hence, once something is uttered, it cannot be un-uttered and can easily spread, by word of mouth, for miles and years.

So, in the same way, the cellphone has a bias toward the caller, not the called. And this means that, sooner or later, and however much we might try to protect ourselves, we will find our accessibility increased.

Whether this is ultimately good or bad for ourselves, our society, our species, remains to be seen. But I suspect it is good. All life thrives on information. Human life especially so, and lack of information, being out of touch, usually breeds misunderstanding and more damage than being in touch too much.

The Internet, independent of the cellphone, opened up vast stores and varieties of information to easy access. The addition of the cellphone means we can access this information, as well as talk to anyone, in the sunshine, on the beach, the mountain peak, or the slick streets in the pounding heart of the city, if we like. The cellphone means we no longer have to choose between information and reality, between conversation and nature. We can have them both. And if we'd rather not, we always can choose to shut the cellphone off, and be no worse off than any other human since the beginning of time.

Select Annotated Bibliography

Agassi, J. (1968). *The Continuing Revolution*. New York: McGraw-Hill.
I have included this book because it introduced me to Johannes Stradanus' sixteenth-century engraving of a contemporary print shop, captioned "Just as one voice can be heard by a multitude of ears, so single writings cover a thousand sheets." (Part of the engraving also appears on the cover of Elizabeth Eisenstein's 1979 work, *The Printing Press as an Agent of Change* [Cambridge, UK: Cambridge University Press]—a generally good historical tract, marred, however, by its summary dismissal, in the preface, of Marshall McLuhan's writing and work as "incoherent.") Back to Stradanus: his caption captures the acoustic quality that the printing press gave to the written word. Before then, each written sheet was single, unique, and readable by just one pair of eyes at a time. A voice, on the other hand, can be heard by numerous ears, simultaneously. It's an organic form of broadcasting, technologically amplified to millions by radio and television. The cellphone and landline telephone before it are significant in part because they are exceptions to this acoustic pattern: only the two people engaged in conversation on the phone are supposed to hear it. When the cellphone performs a bit like radio (and the printing press)—when an audience can overhear at least one side of the conversation—it can become a public nuisance. (Agassi's book, by the way, is worth reading in its entirety. It's a good history of ideas, told by a philosopher of science to his young son, in a series of lessons.)

Anderson, C. (2003). "Cellphones Triggered Bombs, FBI Reports." *Associated Press*, June 12.

Appleton, V. (1914). *Tom Swift and His Photo Telephone*. New York: Grosset & Dunlap.
Most of the thirty-eight books in this popular "young adult" series (today's term for books intended for pre-teen and early teenage readers), beginning with *Tom Swift and His Motorcycle* in 1910, feature real, recently invented technologies—Tom Swift was the "MacGyver" (as in the 1980s television series) of his day. The *Photo Telephone* was a notable exception, providing for "a plate . . . like a mirror, so that any number of images can be made to appear on it . . . . No matter how far two persons may be apart they can both see and talk to one another . . . . Then another thing I want to do is . . . make

a photograph of the person over the wire." The photo telephone, in other words, was even better, more advanced, than a television screen—more like a computer screen, of which printouts can be made. (It is not completely clear if these images were moving or still.) Edward Stratemeyer introduced the Tom Swift character in his 1895 "Shorthand Tom, the Reporter"; Howard R. Garris wrote most of the books ("Appleton" was a fictitious name assigned as author of the novels, regardless of who wrote them.) See also 1911's *Tom Swift and His Wireless Message*, for a nice early adventure in wireless telegraphy.

Asimov, I. (1956). "The Last Question." *Science Fiction Quarterly,* **November.**

In his introduction to one of the many reprints of this story—in *The Edge of Tomorrow* (New York: Tor, 1985)—Asimov says that this is his "favorite story of all of those I have written" (p. 437). A computer is asked if humanity will ever figure out a way of reversing entropy—of increasing the available energy in the universe. It replies that it has insufficient data to answer. In centuries ahead, new, more powerful computers are constructed—which provide the same answer. Humanity fans out to the stars, constructing ever more powerful computers; they each yield the same unyielding answer. In the end—trillions of years later—humanity and the stars are extinguished. Seemingly irreversible entropy has taken its toll. But the all-powerful cosmic computer that remains is at last able to answer the question: it creates light out of darkness, order from entropy. It is God. Computers have been more subject to this apocalyptic kind of fiction than cellphones—and most other media—because computers can give the impression of thinking on their own. (See *The Terminator* movies and *The Matrix* movies for colorful variations on this theme.) My *Mind at Large* (Chapter 7, "Socratic Technology") and *The Soft Edge* (Chapter 18, "Artificial Intelligence in Real Life"), both listed below, explore the extent to which the impression is or may ever be true, and the differences between "autonomous intelligence" (computers think for themselves) and "auxiliary intelligence" (pencils, computers, cellphones extend our intelligence)—two kinds of AI. For the cellphone in fiction, see Dick Tracy's wristwatch and the *Star Trek* communicator.

Bazin, A. (1967). *What Is Cinema?* **trans. H. Gray. Berkeley: University of California Press.**

Useful not only as a history of motion pictures as an attempt to "recreate the world in its own image" (p. 21)—that is, to present the world with sound, color, etc., or the way it is outside of the movie (see also my "anthropotropic" theory of media evolution in "Human Replay," 1979, listed below)—but as an astute assessment of the photograph itself as an image rescued from its "proper corruption" in time (p. 42), free of the "sin" of subjectivity (p. 12). What is at stake here is the difference between abstract communication such as writing and speaking, in which we describe the world in forms that have no resemblance to it, and literal media that bring us the world as it really is. Although speech is itself abstract, its communication via telephone and phonograph provides literal renditions of the sound, and thus make these media (and radio and television) more akin to photography than writing, printing, and the telegraph.

Birkerts, S. (1994). *Gutenberg Elegies: The Fate of Reading in an Electronic Age*. Boston: Faber and Faber.

One of many diatribes that lament the death of literacy—reading, writing, or both—at the hands that hold the ray guns of electronic media. Interestingly, the predominance of the written word on computer screens has made them no less culpable, in this view, than the traditional villain, television (see also Postman, below, for the same). I have two words for Birkerts et al.: Harry Potter.

Brin, D. (1998). *The Transparent Society*. Boston: Addison-Wesley.

A valuable probe and assessment of the loss of privacy at the turn of the new century. Not to be confused, however, with the "telepathic society," discussed in Chapter 4 of the current book, and brought into being by the cellphone. The two societies—transparent and telepathic—overlap, of course, but the telepathic has a crucial element that makes it better and worse, less and more dangerous, than the surveillance, collection of personal data, and the like that characterize Brin's transparent society. Every cellphone transaction in the telepathic society is initiated by someone who is choosing to communicate, making a deliberate decision to do so, not being spied on. That's the good news. The bad news is that receivers of these calls may or may not want to communicate; and refusal to communicate, to be accessible via cellphone, is becoming more and more difficult.

Brooks, J. (1976). *Telephone: The First Hundred Years*. New York: Harper & Row.

An excellent history, chock full of interesting details, especially on the business of the phone. Shortly thereafter, AT&T gave up its near monopoly on phone service—the "divestiture"—and soon the cellphone sprang the phone from the office and home, making Brooks' book something of a monument to a bygone era as well as a history. Has phone service improved, on balance, as a result of the AT&T split-up? Impossible to say, since so many improvements in technology have been introduced in the past few decades. But the thrust of Brooks' book is that AT&T certainly did a fine, important job in its heyday. (I agree, and think, in general, that monopolies or near monopolies in communication often do more good than harm. See Chapter 7 of my *Realspace*, 2003, listed below, for my support of Microsoft against the U.S. government's anti-monopoly charges, and "Senate Panel Votes to Overturn FCC's Eased Media Ownership Rules," *Baltimore Sun*, June 20, 2003, for a quote of my views on the danger to free expression, not from corporate control, but from government attempts to regulate communication.)

Bye Bye Birdie (1959/1963).

The play debuted on Broadway in 1959 for 607 performances; book by Michael Stewart, music by Charles Strouse, lyrics by Lee Adams; it won four Tony Awards. The 1963 movie adaptation by George Sidney did not win any awards (it was nominated for Best Score and Best Sound Oscars), but it has become a classic. This movie is not just an affectionate send-up of Elvis, but a celebration of the phone and teenage sexuality, not coincidentally at the end of the same decade in which the telephone first resided in more than 50 percent of American homes. The opening scene in the movie, with Ann-Margret reclining on her bed, legs crossed and in the air, talking on the phone with friends about boys, is a perfect picture of teenage-girl phone life at this time. (See the postcards discussed in Chapter 7 of this book for snapshots of similar telephone romance earlier in the twentieth century. See Nicholson Baker's 1992 novel, *Vox* [New York: Random House] for a less innocent treatment of the telephone as a vehicle of sex. This was the novel that Monica Lewinsky gave to President Clinton, presumably to commemorate some of their encounters.)

Campbell, D. T. (1974). "Evolutionary Epistemology," in P. A. Schilpp, ed., *The Philosophy of Karl Popper*. La Salle, IL: Open Court.

Articles do not usually receive the recognition given books in the academic world, which is likely why Campbell, whose work was confined to articles, got so little attention. But Campbell's writing in general, and this article in particular, is more important than just about any book in helping us understand the relationship of media, perception, and evolution—in effect, pointing to an intersection of McLuhan and Darwin. (I developed that hybrid in my "Human Replay: A Theory of the Evolution of Media" [listed below], in 1979, about a year before I came across Campbell. I thought so highly of his contribution that I dedicated my 1997 book *The Soft Edge: A Natural History and Future of the Information Revolution*—also listed below—to Campbell, shortly after his death.) The crux of this article (actually, there are more than one) is Campbell's notion of perception as vicarious experience, and its evolutionary benefits. The amoeba—all one-celled organisms—only know of the world what they bump into or touch. If that part of the world happens to be noxious or dangerous, they can die with that truthful perception.

All other forms of perception, with the exception of taste, convey information about the world at a distance, without touching, and are thus safer. We can run away from a fire we see, smell, or hear crackling. But these vicarious modes of experience, like all evolutionary developments, are trade-offs—they are capable of error. The amoeba suffers no optical illusions. Campbell discusses thinking as the most vicarious mode of perception of all, and considers language, human problem-solving, and culture. He briefly looks at computers and their capacity to solve problems. Applying his analysis to media, we can clearly see that the telephone is a vicarious mode of speaking, which the cellphone carries anyplace in the world. The values and drawbacks of this removed form of being in touch are discussed throughout the current book. (See also my extensive discussion of Campbell in *Mind at Large*, listed below. For other applications of Campbell to media evolution, see Paul Kelly's 1997 "Evolutionary Epistemology and Media Evolution," *Journal of Social and Evolutionary Systems* vol. 20, no. 3, and his paper "McLuhan and Darwin," presented at the Fourth Annual Media Ecology Association Conference, Hofstra University, June 7, 2003. Kelly was my student in the Connected Education/OnLine MA in Media Studies Program at the New School in the 1990s, and began his work in this area in his 1997 Masters thesis, "Self-Organization in Media Evolution: A Theoretical Prelude to the Internet.")

Cherry, C. (1985). *The Age of Access: Information Technology and Social Revolution: Posthumous Papers of Colin Cherry*. Compiled and edited by W. Edmondson, Dover, NH: Croom Helm.

Written in the year prior to his death in 1979, Cherry's "A Second Industrial Revolution?" is an unfinished manuscript, begun as part of the work he pursued as a recipient of the Marconi International Fellowship in 1978. Cherry completed three chapters and a series of fragments, all of which are printed here. As Edmondson observes, the book is well situated in time, right on the eve of the personal computer revolution, and (we can now add, but not known in 1985) on the near eve of the cellphonic revolution, too. The book is also well titled—Edmondson explains his choice of "The Age of Access" over "A Second Industrial Revolution" as due not only to Cherry's original title being provisional, but to "the idea of access—instant, far-reaching, probing, invasive" (p. 9) as the most exciting, crucial aspect of the information revolution. It certainly characterizes the cellphone and its impact, and could well have been the title of the current book. (Cherry also touches on a pattern crucial to media evolution and impact, and therefore to the cellphone: the unreliability of experts, including even discoverers of natural phenomena and inventors of technology, as predictors of the application and social acceptance of inventions. Cherry cites the development of radio by

Marconi in the face of pronouncements by Heinrich Hertz, discoverer of electromagnetic waves that make radio work, that use of them for broadcasting would never be possible. Other examples discussed in *Cellphone* include Edison's initial misjudgments of his phonograph and motion pictures; president of Western Union Telegraph William Orton's conviction that the telephone would never be more than a "toy"; and August Comte's view that we would never know the chemical composition of stars. Inventors, of course, sometimes can be right—Jobs and Wozniak certainly saw much of what the personal computer they were developing would make possible. But more often than not, social theorists and philosophers like Marshall McLuhan are more on target than inventors, scientists, and leaders of industry and government with their predictions. Once invented, media are in the hands of the human race, who determine their specific use and success. See my "Human Replay," 1979, listed below, for more.)

Coleridge, S. T. (1817/1907). *Biographia Literaria*, **edited by J. Shawcross. London: Oxford University Press.**

On page 6 Coleridge identifies "that willing suspension of disbelief for the moment, which constitutes poetic faith." Indeed, it constitutes—makes possible—transactions with all media, not just appreciation of poetry. Any communication less than full multisensory seeing, hearing, touching (or permitting touching) is, after all, less than complete, less than real, and in order to take it seriously we must suspend any disbelief we might have about the unreal part, the sector not present. We do this every time we cry at a sad movie or get frightened at a horror show, even though we know full well that neither is real. The phone is probably the easiest coaxer of suspended disbelief, because we are, indeed, conversing with a real person on the other end. But even so, in order for the phone conversation to work, we have to suspend doubt that the person is occupied with someone or something else while talking to us. Videophone would eliminate just about all such doubt. Perhaps we resist it because we value the cover that faceless acoustic phones give us, on one side of the conversation (as potential transgressors—doing something else while talking on the phone), and are willing to rely on poetic faith rather than visual confirmation, on the other side (the side of the doubter).

Darwin, C. (1862/1984). *On the Various Contrivances by which British and Foreign Orchids Are Fertilised by Insects.* **Chicago: University of Chicago Press (reprint edition).**

Certainly not as influential as *The Origin of Species* (1859), but Darwin's very next book, and likely the book Darwin was depicted as looking at in Spike Jonze's 2003 movie *Adaptation* (based loosely on Susan Orleans' novel *The Orchid Thief*, but also a story about Charlie Kaufman, who wrote the screenplay for this film and also for the 1999 movie *Being John Malkovich*, also directed by Jonze). So what does all of this have to do with the cellphone? Well, one of the main objections to Darwin's theory of evolution by natural selection, which posited no Divine organizer or Master watchmaker, was how could highly complex structures like the mammalian eye have evolved without a clear, final goal in mind? What good is a cornea without the rest of the evolved eye? What good is every other part of the eye—none of which can see, unless they function as part of an eye? If we found a watch in the woods, surely we would think that someone deliberately designed it. Why do we not think the same of an eye? Darwin provided an answer in *Orchids*: they attract insects by using parts that were initially evolved for other purposes. The eye, therefore, came together from structures that initially did things other than seeing. Stephen Jay Gould and other evolutionists considered this one of the most important planks for Darwin's theory of natural selection. Its relevance to the cellphone: human thumbs, evolved eons before cellphones to help us grasp, now work perfectly as vehicles of texting on cellphones. (Meanwhile, the movie *Adaptation* is a good example of the contrivances developed for one movie, *Being John Malkovich*, working well in another.)

de Haan, D. (1977). *Antique Household Gadgets and Appliances.* Woodbury, NY: Barron's.

I'm grateful to de Haan for pointing out in this fine little book that "electric lighting did more to improve the habit of reading books than anything before it" (p. 121). Well, perhaps not as much as the printing press, without which there would not have been very many books to read, but it is also true that literacy rates in the United States did not exceed those among citizens of ancient Alexandria until the 1890s, or the advent of electric lighting. Although the most vehement attacks on electronic media as destructive of literacy have been directed against television—see, listed below, Postman's *Technopoly*, 1992, and Wynn's *The Plug-In Drug*, 1977, for examples, and my *The Soft Edge*, 1997, for summaries—they have also been lodged against computers (see Birkerts, 1994, listed above, and Postman) and, most recently, texting on cellphones (see Young, 2003, listed below), media that, like the electric light, facilitate reading and writing. De Haan reminds us that electricity always has been in the service of literacy. Indeed, the first technological use of electricity was in the telegraph, also a literate medium. (De Haan's observation also calls attention to the home as a center of communication with the world, a state of affairs strengthened by the telephone and television and their need of wires and power available only indoors. Books became more readable in homes, in evenings, with electric lights. Transistor radios and now cellphones reversed this pattern, and bring centers of communication outdoors.)

Dewey, John (1925). *Experience and Nature.* Chicago: Open Court.

Unique, uncommunicated events and ideas "tremble on the verge of disappearance" (p. 148); communication, then, makes life fully real. Regarded by many as the greatest American philosopher of the twentieth century, Dewey might have seen the cellphone as dramatically increasing the endurance, impact, and reality of ideas, feelings, and personal experiences, by making their communication to people anywhere in the world, anytime, so easy. The "verge of disappearance" also can apply to words written on computer screens—and, for that matter, to words spoken, whether in person or on the phone—in contrast to words permanently affixed to paper. But the fleeting contents of computer screens tend to keep people indoors, where the electric power and connections are more reliable and what is on the screen can be better safeguarded. This can limit communication, certainly interpersonal exchanges with many people. In contrast, the words spoken on cellphones, while also fleeting, can be spoken outdoors and indoors, anywhere there may be other people with whom we may want to converse. The net effect of the cellphone, then, unlike the indoor computer, is to increase the opportunities for communication across the board—with people close at hand as well as far away. (Laptops and Palm Pilots have the same salutary effect, but they are used much less than cellphones.)

Dunnewind, S. (2003). " 'Generation Text': Teens' IM Lingo Evolving into a Hybrid Language." *Seattle Times,* June 11.

Eder, J. M. (1945/1978). *History of Photography.* New York: Columbia University/Dover.

A highly detailed, step-by-step account of the first century of photography and its prelude. (The 1978 Dover edition is a reprint, not an update, so this history ends in 1945.)

Emery, M., and Emery, E. (1992). *The Press and America: An Interpretive History of the Mass Media,* 7th ed. Englewood Cliffs, NJ: Prentice-Hall.

The best history of the press in America I have come across, meticulously and comprehensively researched, rich with interesting detail, alert throughout to the role of new technologies. Both Emerys—father (Edwin) and son (Michael)—died prior to the publication of the eighth edition in 1995 by Allyn & Bacon. This publisher also brought out a ninth edition in 1999, coauthored by Nancy Roberts, a colleague of Michael Emery at the University of Minnesota; it contains expanded sections on all-news cable television. I hope there is a tenth edition, which could not help but deal with embedded journalists in the 2003 Iraqi War and how cellphones with videophone connections enabled them.

Family Safe Media (2003). "Pornography Statistics, 2003." Published on the Web at www.familysafemedia.com/pornography_statistics.html.

This site publishes current economic statistics on pornography, which, as of 2003, grossed $57 billion worldwide and $12 billion in the United States. Phone sex accounted for $4.5 billion of that worldwide, followed by $2.5 billion for cable and pay-per-view television, and $2.5 billion for the Internet—which would likely be much more, except for the fact that so much of everything on the Web is provided free. For that matter, there is likely a lot of unmetered talking about sex on the phone, as well. Family Safe Media, it must be noted, is against pornography, and thus these statistics are probably in the higher range of estimate. Still, by any counting, there is a lot of sex on the telephone. (No statistics that I have come across distinguish sex on cellphones from sex on landline phones. But the cellphone is no doubt sexual in a variety of ways, including its use as a vibrator, reported by Rothman, "Gadget of the Week," below.)

Freud, S. (1930/1961). *Civilization and Its Discontents*, trans. J. Riviere/ J. Strachey. New York: Cape and Smith/Norton.

Sometimes all a book needs to be extraordinarily important is a single, uniquely apt sentence, or even a phrase. This book—and, of course, Freud's work in general—is extraordinarily important for numerous reasons, but, over the years, I have found one phrase, which, if the book contained nothing else of value, would still make it one of the fundamental texts of media theory and our understanding of the role of the written word in human history: "Writing," Freud notes on page 38, "was in its origin the voice of an absent person." That really says it all. A voice can be absent for two reasons: space (too far away, in physical, geographic distance) or time (the listener arrives after or before the voice has spoken), or both. Nothing can be done about future voices becoming available in the present, short of communicating backward in time, which so far does not seem possible. (Communication, like life and physical existence, moves only forward in time.) Regarding literal retrieval of lost voices, that first became possible with Edison's phonograph in 1877, and started to become so for people everywhere, on the move, with the cassette players of the 1970s. Telephone and radio first allowed voices absent because of long distance to be heard in the home. (Telephone voices are interactive; radio voices go just one-way.) Cellphones now allow conversations with voices absent for reasons of distance, from anywhere the two speakers happen to be. The upshot: Were someone through the magic of time travel able to go back to the prehistoric Cro-Magnon and possibly Neanderthal places where writing was first invented and give these people a gift of an endless supply of cellphones and cassette (or now, CD) portable players, we might now all well be illiterate.

Fuller, B. (1939). *Nine Chains to the Moon.* Carbondale: Southern Illinois University Press.

A decade before the transistor shrank the vacuum tube in 1948, Fuller saw a "dymaxion principle" in the development of technology: it progresses by doing more with physically less. The microchip and the digital revolution it engendered are the current jewels in the dymaxion crown. Among many other advantages, they make lots of things portable, since ever-more-powerful chips weigh next to nothing. At the same time, however, at the other end of the technological continuum, the natural human brain may be the greatest dymaxion triumph of all: Think of all that we do and can imagine with the kilogram of matter in our skulls. (Fuller, along with Freeman Dyson, is also among the very few philosophers who see human intelligence working through technology as capable of not only overcoming entropy—the tendency of all things to run down, lose energy, dissipate, die—but eventually reversing the universal process of entropy completely. I thoroughly agree. I would put the matter as follows: Entropy may well be an infinite down escalator, which no amount of our running upward can surmount, but with our intelligence and technology we may well figure out a way of getting at the very mechanism of the escalator and make *it* run upward. See my *Mind at Large*, 1988, listed below, for more.)

Granick, H. (1947/1991). *Underneath New York.* New York: Henry Holt & Company (1947 edition); New York: Fordham University Press (1991 edition, with introduction by R. E. Sullivan, Jr.).

A rich, delightful source of detail about the telecommunication infrastructure in New York City in the first half of the twentieth century, with chapters "Chute the Mail!" (on pneumatic tubes, which of course were physical not electronic, but they nonetheless delivered mail to many places much faster than by hand), "Don't Write, Telegraph!" and "Hello! Telephone." We learn that an ice storm "in 1909 caused the head of AT&T to order long distance cables underground. That storm carried away the overhead telephone circuits through which the New York City Press was expecting to hear the eyewitness accounts of the inauguration of a new President of the United States, William H. Taft" (p. 142). Cellphones, which do away with cables completely, are of course a better solution.

Greenspan, R. (2003). "Look Who's Talking, Texting, Buying." *CyberAtlas*, March 25, cyberatlas.internet.com/markets/wireless/print.

Heinlein, R. (1966). *The Moon Is a Harsh Mistress.* New York: Putnam/ Berkley.

A classic, relatively rare example of a heroic, self-sacrificing computer in science fiction. Most of the time, when computers and robots have minds of their own, they are outright enemies of their human creators (or of a humanity that did not create them), or deeply ambiguous in their relationship to us. Asimov's robots are another exception, but even they often contrive, by intention or otherwise, to do us almost as much harm as good. (See, for example, Asimov's *The Robots of Dawn* [New York: Doubleday, 1983] and *Robots and Empire* [New York: Doubleday, 1985].)

Hitler, A. (1924/1971). *Mein Kampf,* **trans. R. Manheim. Boston: Houghton Mifflin (reprint edition).**

He dislikes the written word, claiming that "all great, world-shaking events have been brought about, not by the written matter, but by the spoken word . . . . the speaker gets a continuous correction of his speech from the crowd he is addressing, since he can always see in the face of his listeners to what extent they can follow his arguments . . . [but] the writer does not know his readers at all" (p. 469). Yet Hitler nonetheless chose to write and publish this point, as did Plato of Socrates, who presented essentially the same argument in the *Phaedrus* (listed below) some 2,400 years earlier. Hitler also used radio broadcasts facilitated by his Minister of Popular Enlightenment and Propaganda, Joseph Goebbels, and movies made by Leni Riefenstahl, neither of which allowed him to see his audiences. But radio allowed him to directly address the German people, unfiltered and unfettered by journalistic quoting and paraphrasing and editorial decision (disliked by Hitler even when made by newspapers under Nazi control). The embedded journalist reporting live with a cellphone from a war zone can have the same effect, but with just the opposite political consequences: to the degree that live, cellphonic reports are not controlled or censored by the government, they can be the most truthful, democratic reporting of a war in history. See Chapter 10 in the current volume, for examples from the 2003 Iraqi War.

Hogarth, S. H. (1926). "Three Great Mistakes." *Blue Bell,* **November.**

The mistakes were Chauncey M. Depew's (1834–1924), New York financier and politician, who declined an offer to purchase one-sixth of all Bell Telephone stock, into perpetuity, for the sum of $10,000 in 1881, after having been advised by his friend, William Orton, president of Western Union Telegraph, that the telephone would never be anything more than a "toy." The potential of new media has been systematically misjudged for centuries by everyone ranging from inventors to investors. In the past decade, the biggest mis-assessment was the over-estimation of the Internet—or, at least, the amount of time people were willing to spend, the amount of business they were willing to conduct, the amount of pleasure they wanted to pursue, seated at a desk in front of a screen. That inflation of the stationary Internet is now being corrected by the cellphone. And what were Depew's other two mistakes? He decided not to pursue what would have been an almost certain nomination as the Republican candidate for president in 1888, thinking the Democratic incumbent, Grover Cleveland, was certain to be reelected. Depew withdrew his bid in favor of Benjamin Harrison, who went on to win the presidency on the Republican line that year. (In all fairness to Depew, however, Cleveland did win the popular vote—Harrison won in the Electoral College—so Depew's judgment was not completely off.) But his third mistake was a doozy: Depew waited until he was thirty-eight years of age to marry, because he wanted to have at least $50,000 saved before committing to such a responsibility. He lost his life savings shortly after marriage and later said he always lamented those long years of bachelorhood. (He did manage, however, to serve as U.S. Senator from New York from 1899 to 1911—an appointed, not an elected, position in those days.)

Huff, R. (2003). "CNN's Own 'Devil Doc' Scrubs Up for Duty Again." *New York Daily News*, April 9.

Innis, H. (1951). *The Bias of Communication*. Toronto: University of Toronto Press.

This and Innis' earlier book, *Empire and Communications* (1950, same publisher), are gratefully acknowledged by Marshall McLuhan as one of his greatest influences and inspirations (the other would be James Joyce). Innis' central point—from which, one could aptly argue, all future media theory including McLuhan's derives—is that all media have "biases" toward either "space-binding" (movement of information across distance) or "time-binding" (movement of information across time), and that the dominant communication bias in any society shapes political and social events. Thus, the media of ancient Egypt were mostly hieroglyphics, which took a long time to learn and were affixed to unmoving walls. This time bias resulted in a profoundly conservative, hierarchical society, highly resistant to any change. In contrast, Rome relied on a quickly acquired alphabet, written on codices that were easy to carry long distances on Roman roads. The result was a rapidly changing, iconoclastic society, moving from pagan republic to pagan empire to Christian empire in less than half a millennium. McLuhan developed Innis' space and time biases into sensory tendencies, with often surprising results: print is biased toward the eye, but all electronic media, including television, have an acoustic bias, because they can be in all places at once, like a sound, and unlike what we look at in the natural world, which needs to be in front of us to be seen. I pointed out in "McLuhan's Space," 1990, and *Digital McLuhan*, 1999—both listed below—that cyberspace is also acoustic. In the current book, I argue that the bias of the cellphone is toward accessibility—whatever we may do to insulate ourselves, we are fighting an uphill battle against a world in which everyone is reachable—and this is, in large part, because we greatly value being able to reach other people when we want to.

Kageyama, Y. (2003). "Camera-Equipped Phones Spread Mischief." Associated Press, July 9.

Marketed world-wide in 2003, the cellphone with camera attachment has become an instant, textbook case of unintended consequences in media evolution. In addition to happy snapshots of the kids sent at lightning e-mail speed to Grandma a continent away, new digital-camera phones are being used to secretly take photos of people in locker rooms and bathrooms. Kageyama reports that "one culprit was fined $4,200" in Japan for taking "photos up the skirts of unsuspecting women in crowded trains and stores." The fines have apparently done little to stop the practice. A Yahoo search in November 2003 for "upskirt" + "photos" yields more than 400,000 hits. Some of these are advertised as "posed," and some that are advertised as "unposed" are no doubt posed, but nonetheless . . .

Kipling, R. (1904). "The Wireless." *Traffics and Discoveries*, **reprinted in B. Adler, Jr., ed.** *Time Machines*. **New York: Carroll & Graff, 1998.**

The ghost of John Keats writes via wireless telegraphy to a man dying of consumption on a stormy night at the beginning of the twentieth century. Science fiction offers not only speculation about future technologies, but telling glimpses into how new technologies were first perceived in the past, shortly before or after their introduction. Kipling's little story speaks of the cosmic possibilities, the sheer magic, people felt when they first contemplated wireless communication—or communication through nothing, through everywhere, and therefore from nothing and everywhere, at the same time. The cellphone debuted in the popular culture of Dick Tracy's walkie-talkie wristwatch, the 1954 movie *Sabrina* (in which the millionaire character played by Humphrey Bogart talks on his car phone), and *Star Trek*'s "communicator," into which Captain Kirk said "Beam me up, Scotty" so many times. (See listing below for *Star Trek*; see also *Tom Swift* by "Appleton," 1914, listed above, for early science fiction about the videophone.)

Lamb, G. (2003). "New take-it-with-you numbers." *The Christian Science Monitor*, **November 17.**

I observed in this article that "what may well happen is that the cellphone number may replace the Social Security number as the most universally given numerical identification." And, indeed, the FCC ruling in the United States in November 2003 to allow people to retain their cellphone numbers from carrier to carrier, and from landlines to cellphones, has accentuated a growing sense of personal identification that people have with their cellphone numbers. Just as social security numbers have been used for many kinds of identification having nothing to do with retirement—such as student IDs at universities—cellphone numbers may gradually take over this role. But they will be "smart" social security numbers, which not only identify their owners but provide a way that they can be contacted.

Leinster, M. (1946). "A Logic Named Joe." *Astounding Science Fiction,* **March.**

Identified by Isaac Asimov as the first science story about a "home"—or personal—computer (I. Asimov, C. G. Waugh, and M. H. Greenberg, *Isaac Asimov Presents the Best Science Fiction Firsts* [New York: Barnes & Noble, 1984/1996]; Leinster's story is reprinted in this volume). In general, science fiction missed the personal computer revolution, and during the 1940s, 1950s, and 1960s was much more interested in big mainframe computers that controlled the world (see Asimov's "The Last Question" and Robert Heinlein's *Moon Is a Harsh Mistress,* listed above) or in robots that walked among us (see all of Asimov's robot stories, especially *The Caves of Steel* [New York, Doubleday, 1953] and *The Naked Sun* [New York: Doubleday, 1956]). The cellphone continues more in the robot than the "home" computer tradition, since, like robots, cellphones get out in the world—but unlike robots, *we* do the talking with the cellphone. (Significantly, Leinster heralds the personal, home computer just a year after Vannevar Bush's famous "As We May Think" article in the July 1945 *Atlantic Monthly,* which predicts the installment on our desks of a little "memex" machine, through which we can write, store, send, receive, and retrieve documents from and to anywhere in the world.)

Levinson, P. (1977). "Toy, Mirror, and Art: The Metamorphosis of Technological Culture." *et cetera,* **vol. 34, no. 2.**

My first major published article, reprinted four times, the most prominent being in Larry Hickman, ed., *Technology as a Human Affair* [New York: McGraw-Hill, 1990]. Traces the developmental stages—childhood, adolescence, adulthood—of technologies. New media enter the world as toys, as gimmicks to amaze and amuse. At first no one cares about their content. People initially talked on the phone just for the thrill of it; Edison's most successful early motion picture was *Fred Ott's Sneeze*—the story of which was, well, Mr. Ott sneezing. As people grow more accustomed to the technology, just the reverse occurs: the technique becomes invisible, people suspend their disbelief (see Coleridge, discussed above), and react to or interact with the content as if it is real. The more we talk on the phone, the more we are drawn into the conversation, the less we usually are aware that we are talking on a phone to someone miles away. In movie theaters, we begin crying, laughing, shivering in response to what we see on the screen, as if it really were happening. The technology is now in the second, or mirror-of-reality, phase. Sometimes media go on to a third stage, in which they not only reflect reality but rearrange and reconfigure it. Editing in motion pictures, first physical, now digital, shows us things and events that may look real, but are not. The director is able to piece together images that have no connection in the real world, to make new realities on the screen. Film in this mature stage has progressed from mirror to art. In what stage is the cellphone? Nowadays, the speed of technological innovation makes the toy stage, the childhood of any medium, all too brief. Most people get over the thrill of talking on the cellphone in weeks or less; after you have "texted" four or five times, it seems, if not old hat, certainly just another useful way of communicating. Will talking on the cellphone become an art? That is a tough order in a medium that has no editing, no easy way to get beyond the mirror. Perhaps phone sex is a kind of art, or using conversation on the phone to go a bit beyond the reality at hand.

Levinson, P. (1979). "Human Replay: A Theory of the Evolution of Media." Ph.D. dissertation, New York University.

I present and develop my "anthropotropic" theory of media evolution here ("anthropo" = human; "tropic" = toward), which argues that, contrary to critics of media who contend that they are making our communication and lives artificial, media actually provide increasingly human, natural, "pretechnological" modes of communication. I describe three phases of media evolution: In Stage A, all communication depends upon biological modes of perception and cognition, such as eyes, ears, memories, and imaginations, and can go only so far as these organs and processes allow. On the plus side, however, every aspect of the natural world capable of our immediate perception can be part of our communication. Nonetheless, driven to do better than our memories, to make real some of what we see and hear in our imaginations, we invent technologies of communication such as writing, which allow us to communicate far beyond biological boundaries, through both space and time. We have reached a new level, Stage B. But we pay a price for the advantages of this new stage: writing loses the sound, color, imagery, three-dimensionality of the real world. Indeed, in order to communicate long distance and across time through writing, the author must leave everything behind except the thought and the abstract description. This Stage B trade-off creates pressure for better media that allow us to communicate beyond biological boundaries without the loss of the natural world. Telephone thus allows us to converse with voices rather than Morse code; radio gives us news in spoken words rather than writing; television brings us ever more lifelike images—we have entered Stage C, a realm of technology that gives us the best of everything, allows us to partake of long distance, permanent communication, and still have the cake of the natural world. The cellphone is clearly an archangel of this new, still-incomplete realm. Back in 1979, I forecast the advent and impact of the cellphone as follows: "the wireless, portable evolution of media should continue to the point of providing any individual with access to all the information of the planet, from anyplace on the planet, indoors and outdoors, and of course even beyond the planet itself, as communication extends into the solar system and cosmos beyond. Radios in automobiles, and movies in airplanes, are but the modest beginnings" (pp. 275–76).

Levinson, P. (1980). "Benefits of Watching Television." *ERIC* microfiche, #ED 233404.

One of my lesser-known papers—likely because it was never published, but presented to a faculty colloquium at Fairleigh Dickinson University in Teaneck, New Jersey, where I taught at the time. Here I argue that watching television can encourage literacy, as when viewers decide to read a book they have seen dramatized on TV. But my most important point is that television is good for us, precisely because it requires so little of us. A certain amount of off time, a medium that entertains us while allowing us to fall asleep in front of it, may be healthy for us in this stressful world. (Charles "Chip" McGrath—then, and as of November 2003, editor of the *New York Times Sunday Book Review*, made a similar point two decades later in his "Giving Saturday Morning Some Slack," *New York Times Magazine*, November 9, 1997.)

Levinson, P. (1988). *Mind at Large: Knowing in the Technological Age.* Greenwich, CT: JAI Press.

The key point of this book is that all technologies are embodiments of human ideas. The automobile, for example, is a veritable compendium of ideas, turned into constructions of metal, rubber, glass, and so on, about how to move, how to ride comfortably, how to see out of a moving vehicle. Taken as a whole, then, human technologies offer a super Library of Congress, a tangible record and literal expression of ideas that have worked, at least insofar as they were capable of being embodied and implemented in physical structures. From such a perspective, communication technologies can be seen as conveying ideas in two ways: A book not only tells the story in its pages, but, whatever that story may be, the book is also an expression of the idea to communicate via writing and printing in bound paper pages, in contrast to say, telling the same story orally, or broadcasting it on radio, or making a movie of it. The cellphone similarly packs a double punch of communication: what is said or written through it, and the fact that one can do this from just about any place in the world, any time, via the cellphone. (This last point follows from McLuhan's "the medium is the message," or, the *what* of communication may not be as important as the *how*; see McLuhan's *Understanding Media*, listed below.) (*Mind at Large* also contains extensive discussions of what I call "never dogmatism" in the history of thought, science, and invention; pre-adaptation in biological and technological evolution; and other themes dealt with and drawn upon in *Cellphone*.)

Levinson, P. (1989). "Intelligent Writing: The Electronic Liberation of Text." *Technology in Society* vol. 11, no. 3, pp. 387–400. Reprinted in Michael Fraase, *Hypermedia, Volume Two*, Chicago: Scott, Foresman, 1990, and Paul Levinson, *Learning Cyberspace*, San Francisco: Anamnesis, 1995.

"I cannot help feeling, Phaedrus, that writing is unfortunately like painting; for the creations of the painter have the attitude of life, and yet if you ask them a question, they preserve a solemn silence. And the same can be said of [written] speeches. You would imagine that they had intelligence, but if you want to know anything and put a question to one of them, the 'speaker' gives but one unvarying answer . . . . [But] may we not imagine another kind of writing or speaking far better than this, and having far greater power? . . . I am speaking of an intelligent writing which . . . can defend itself, and knows when to speak and when to be silent," Socrates says to Phaedrus, according to Plato in his dialogue of that name, sections 275–276 (see listing below). In "Intelligent Writing" I argue that words written on computers, connected to the Internet with its e-mail, group discussion, and hypertext facilities, fulfills precisely this Socratic request. Texting on cellphones may do this even more efficiently, since cellphones permit talking in text outdoors as well as indoors, and without lengthy log-on procedures. ("Intelligent Writing" also answers critics of electronic media and computers, who contend that these media disable literacy—see Birkerts, listed above, and Postman, listed below. Also see Young, listed below, for a vitriolic denunciation of texting as antithetical to traditional writing.)

Levinson, P. (1990). "McLuhan's Space." *Journal of Communication* 40, no. 2. Review of Philip Marchand, *Marshall McLuhan: The Medium and the Messenger* (New York: Ticknor & Fields, 1989); Marshall McLuhan and Eric McLuhan, *Laws of Media* (Toronto: University of Toronto Press, 1988); Marshall McLuhan and Bruce Powers, *The Global Village* (New York: Oxford University Press, 1989); Matie Molinaro, Corinne McLuhan, and William Toye, eds. *Letters of Marshall McLuhan* (New York: Oxford University Press, 1988). (Marshall McLuhan died in 1980; the above books with his coauthorship were published posthumously.)

I argue in this essay/review that McLuhan's work—from his first published book (*The Mechanical Bride*, 1951) through his essays in the 1950s in the journal *Explorations* through his discussion of "the global village" in *The Gutenberg Galaxy* in 1962 (see listing below) and all that came after could be seen as a recognition of a new communication environment that had just begun to come into being. It was the environment of instant, omnipresent electronic media, which started by bringing us short, clipped telegrams, progressed to sounds via telephone and radio, and by the 1950s was providing us with images and sounds via television. McLuhan strove to understand it, and grappled even with what to call it. He settled, pretty much, on "acoustic space" (a term that apparently first surfaced in McLuhan and Edmund Carpenter's seminars at the University of Toronto in 1954 and was the title of an article published a year later under their byline in *Explorations*), because sounds, like electronic media, approach us from all parts of the environment, from a 360-degree circumference around our heads. In "McLuhan's Space" I said that acoustic space was none other than cyberspace, which, courtesy of e-mail, online communication, and the then-nascent Internet, had now come much more fully into existence. My *Digital McLuhan*, 1999—listed below—developed this theme. The growing importance of the cellphone, however, suggests that "acoustic" may well be a better appellation for this space, after all. Not only does the cellphone convey spoken words, but it is increasingly subsuming aspects of cyberspace, as in "texting." Indeed, one of the theses of the current book is that, in the long run, the Internet and cyberspace will function as vassals of the cellphone.

Levinson, P. (1992). "Icons and Garbage Cans," in P. Levinson, *Electronic Chronicles: Columns of the Changes in our Times*. San Francisco: Anamnesis Press.

I actually wrote and first published this—and most of the *Electronic Chronicles*—in the mid-1980s, as part of an online weekly commentary (something like what we would today call a "blog") for the Western Behavioral Sciences Institute, where (in cyberspace, along with two yearly, in-person meetings) I had also been teaching online since 1984. In this little essay, I complain that icons and clickable images are less supple and thus less powerful than good, old-fashioned alphabetic commands—that is, commands that draw upon the efficacy of our language. I wrote this prior to the advent of the Web, as an argument on behalf of DOS versus Macintosh command systems. The Web clearly went the way of the clickable icon. But it is worth noting that everything from e-mail to listservs to blogs still runs on alphabetic text. Meanwhile, though texting on cellphones certainly is well sprinkled with smiley faces and like emoticons, it also—apropos its name—is a system of text, which requires, encourages, and is facilitated by literacy.

Levinson, P. (1992). "The Nine Lives of Electronic Text," in P. Levinson, *Electronic Chronicles: Columns of the Changes in our Times.* San Francisco: Anamnesis Press.

The digital revolution has had contradictory effects on the reliability (and survivability) of text. On the one hand, just as the printing press saved books from the dangers of all being in one basket, with unique copies of manuscripts lost when the Library of Alexandria was burned, so has electronic dissemination of text made it immune to permanent loss from any deliberate or accidental erasure. On the other hand, electronic text is easier to erase than a printed book, and, even more worrisome, it is easily amenable to unauthorized or deceptive alteration. (The same is true of digital photography.) In this brief essay from the mid-1980s (see my "Icons and Garbage Cans," listed above, for details on the publication of the essays in *Electronic Chronicles*), I discuss the ironic difficulty, given the way personal computers process data, of permanently erasing electronic text: "Erasure" and "deletions" usually remove just the computer's internal listing of the file, so that it can be written over, at some time when the RAM (random access memory) alights on that part of the disk. But before that time, the text is not actually erased, which means it can be retrieved. (More sophisticated "burn" commands can banish the unwanted text more effectively.) In cyberspace, then, things are easier to both erase *and* retrieve. The cellphone contributes to both sides of this complex balance: Spoken conversations, like nontechnological speech itself, usually are gone the instant they are uttered; text messages easily can endure in an "Inbox" on the cellphone. But this could change rather quickly in favor of preservation and retrieval, if we wished to have cellphones that recorded all spoken conversations.

Levinson, P. (1992). "Samizdat Video Revisited," in P. Levinson, *Electronic Chronicles: Columns of the Changes in our Times.* San Francisco: Anamnesis Press.

This essay was written after most of the other *Chronicles*—after the dissolution of the Soviet Union—and argues that small, personal, handheld or easily operated communications media are inherently subversive to big, centralized governments. This was true of both the nascent photocopier, used by the "White Rose" to print and disseminate anti-Nazi material during Hitler's reign, and the portable video camera in the Soviet Union in the 1980s. Unfortunately, the same decentralizing capacity—prevalent today in cellphones, Palm Pilots, and laptops—can be wielded easily by terrorists. (This, alas, was not yet obvious in 1992—just a year before the first World Trade Center bombing.) For details on the "White Rose," see A. E. Dumbach and J. Newborn, *Shattering the German Night* (Boston: Little, Brown, 1986). For more on new media as terrorist instruments, see my *Realspace*, 2003, listed below, Chapter 11 ("Realspace in an Age of Terrorism"). And on yet another hand, see Chapter 10 ("The Cellphone at War") in the current book for discussion of the cellphone as an instrument of war against terrorist nations.

Levinson, P. (1993). "The Amish Get Wired—The Amish?" *Wired*, vol. 1, no. 6, p. 124. Contrary to the view of the Amish in our popular culture as Luddites, they do not simply reject all new technology out of hand, but rather pick and choose, on the basis of how a new technology might help them without disrupting their way of life. As an example, they do not want telephones in the home, but years before the cellphone, some Amish constructed "phone shacks"—private phone booths, of sorts—on the edges of their property, for occasions when they wanted to make a call. And although they resist being beholden to central power companies, many have no problem with electronic devices—including personal computers—operated via batteries. I first noticed this, with my own eyes, during several trips I took with my family to Strasburg in Lancaster County, Pennsylvania, in the late 1980s, and I wrote about it in "A New York Philosopher in Amish County," first published online and then in my *Electronic Chronicles: Columns of the Changes in Our Times*, San Francisco: Anamnesis, 1992. "The Amish Get Wired"—my second of six small essays published in *Wired*—was a nice pun, given the name of the publication, but a bit confusing, since the thrust of my piece was that the Amish wherever possible preferred wireless, battery-operated devices. (My original title for this essay was "Digital Amish"; it was changed to "The Amish Get Wired" by *Wired*.) Not surprisingly, then, many Amish have snapped up the cellphone. (Howard Rheingold details this in "Look Who's Talking," *Wired*, vol. 7, no. 1, 1999—which unfortunately is written as if he was the first to discover the "secret love affair" the Amish are having with some technology.) (For those who like fiction: The Amish and their technology are the main theme of my science fiction novelette, "The Mendelian Lamp Case," featuring NYPD forensic detective Dr. Phil D'Amato—first published in *Analog*, April 1997, and reprinted four times, including David Hartwell, ed., *Year's Best SF #3*, 1998. This story also serves as the first section of my novel, *The Silk Code* [New York: Tor, 1999], where the Amish play a continuing, significant role.)

Levinson, P. (1996). "On Behalf of Humanity: The Technological Edge." *The World and I*, March, pp. 300–13. Reprinted in P. Levinson, *Bestseller: Wired, Analog, and Digital Writings*. Mill Valley, CA: Pulpless, 1999.

Presents my "Guns, Knives, and Pillows" analysis—or the futile search for an intrinsically always good or always bad technology. Guns, after all, can be used to hunt food, which if it keeps us from starving, is good. The innocuous pillow on which we rest our head can be an instrument of murder, through suffocation—bad. Moreover, even our understanding of radiation and atomic energy, which led to the atom bomb, has been applied to medicine (good), just as medical technologies have been used to create biological weapons (bad). In the end, then, all technologies are different versions of knives, which can be used for good (to cut food) or bad (to cut people)—even though many technologies, like guns and pillows, have a bias toward bad or good. (See Innis, *The Bias of Communication*, listed above, for more on "biases" of technology.) The cellphone, however, is a two-edged sword of technology par excellence, with biases right down the middle, to help (give us access to other people) and hurt (give other people access to us, when we would prefer not). This is what makes the cellphone so interesting a subject of study.

Levinson, P. (1997). *The Soft Edge: A Natural History and Future of the Information Revolution*. London & New York: Routledge.

Scant attention to the cellphone here, but *The Soft Edge* does offer extensive discussion of some of its most important roots, including (of course) the social impact of the telephone and radio. The book presents, in effect, a picture of the past and future of the digital revolution, from the vantage point of the first (and thus far, only) peak of Web life and cyberspace. Much of what I observed from that place is still true, subject to some of that now being channeled through the cellphone. (And see also my *Realspace*, 2003, listed below, for the importance of transportation and face-to-face communication in human life and progress.)

Levinson, P. (1999). *Digital McLuhan: A Guide to the Information Millennium*. London & New York: Routledge.

Makes two related points: (1) McLuhan's work, confusing and infuriating to many in the 1960s, became more comprehensible, rang true to more people, in the 1990s, because it was all along addressing an electronic media world that did not come fully, or at least not more than embryonically, into being until the digital revolution; and (2) McLuhan's observations from the 1950s through the 1970s indeed provide the best guide for understanding the world of cable television, personal computers, and the Web. The aspects of McLuhan's work most relevant to the cellphone are his focus on "acoustic space" (see Levinson, 1990, "McLuhan's Space," listed above) and the changing role of the telephone (see McLuhan, *Understanding Media*, 1964, and his "Inside on the Outside," 1976, listed below). Both themes are treated extensively in *Digital McLuhan*, but the cellphone only gets glancing reference, and mostly in its initial incarnation as a "car phone" (p. 134).

Levinson, P. (2003). *Realspace: The Fate of Physical Presence in the Digital Age, On and Off Planet*. London & New York: Routledge.

This short book explores our need to get out of our seats, from behind our screens, away from cyberspace and back into the real world of movement, transport, and communication with flesh-and-blood people. Here the cell-phone makes a major appearance, in its own chapter, "The Cellphone as Antidote to the Internet." In the current book, however, I further consider not only how the cellphone helps us get out of our homes and offices and back out in the big, wide world, but also how the cellphone's demands on our accessibility can curtail our freedom to roam through this world, and transform it into one big office or den if we are not careful. (*Realspace* also considers our need to physically move off of this planet and explore, live, and work in worlds beyond our own—a profound issue, dealing with questions of human spirituality, philosophy, as well as science, and distinct from the cellphone—although the capacity to call back home never hurts.)

Lippmann, W. (1922). *The Phantom Public.* **New York: Macmillan.**

Lippmann sours on American democracy in this classic and influential book, because the public is uninformed and apathetic, rendering their electoral choices meaningless. The book was published on the eve of radio's emer-gence as a mass medium for delivery of news—followed in subsequent decades by television, by 24/7 all-news cable television, and by the Internet, not only a vehicle of news, but a place for public and private discussion of news with people other than those in the same room. So are we better informed, more fit for and deserving of democracy, at least by Lippmann's lights? Difficult to say. And maybe uninformed opinion is not so inimical to the democratic process. Cellphones certainly have made talking about political issues easier, and were said to help mobilize some of the ineffective rallies against the Iraqi War in 2003, but there is no hard data on their polit-ical impact, at least in the United States, that I know of. (But see Rheingold's *Smart Mobs*, 2003—listed below—for discussion of some of the cellphone's reported political impact overseas, especially the Philippines, where crowds brought together by text messages pressured President Joseph Estrada to step down in 2001.)

Maddox, B. (1972). *Beyond Babel.* **New York: Simon & Schuster.**

A good account of the state of telecommunications in 1972, including the half century of unfulfilled promise of the videophone. "Perhaps the demand will materialize," she remarks, doubtfully, on p. 208. In 2003, the use of cell-phones with videophone attachments by embedded reporters in the Iraqi War, and the sale of inexpensive cellphones with photographic and video clip (but not live video transmission) features, show that perhaps such material-ization is at last close at hand (though, as Maddox pointed out, and has been the case since her assessment, the videophone has never seemed very far from hand, and nonetheless has yet to be adopted for daily, commonplace conversation—as has the cellphone).

Maeroff, G. (1978). "Reading Achievement in Indiana Found as Good as in '44." *The New York Times*, April 15.

Mander, J. (1978). *Four Arguments for the Elimination of Television*. New York: Morrow.

Included simply as the most preposterous of the many critiques offered against television—in this case, that watching it may cause cancer. Mander, a former advertising executive when he wrote this tract, suffered from what I call the "repentant electrocutioner" complex: if you want to know about the morality of electricity, don't ask a former electrocutioner. See my review of this book in *The Structurist* 19/20 (1979/1980), for more.

McCullough, D. (1992). *Truman*. New York: Simon & Schuster.

According to McCullough, Truman didn't like the phone (p. 141). He was the last president not to embrace new media—JFK installed the hot line between Washington and Moscow, Clinton's vice president Al Gore championed the Internet in the 1990s—and indeed most presidents before Truman also were quick to see the value in new technologies of communication. Lincoln allowed Mathew Brady to photograph the Civil War, and communicated with Grant in the field via telegraph. Franklin Delano Roosevelt was a master of radio. But, come to think of it, Eisenhower never cared for the space program—he called it "pie in the sky." Something about those late 1940s and 1950s— maybe the immediate aftermath of the atom bomb, maybe the pace of technology going too fast for those last two twentieth-century presidents born in the nineteenth century (as JFK was happy to point out about Eisenhower in his 1961 inauguration speech)—made them wary of technology.

McKeever, W. (1910). "Motion Pictures: A Primary School for Criminals." *Good Housekeeping*, August, pp. 184–86.

Sometimes doing research can be as painstaking as relaxing at a country auction on a summer's evening, where I found this issue of *Good Housekeeping* at the bottom of a box of old magazines I had purchased for a few dollars. McKeever's article—forgotten, as far as I could tell, until I mentioned it in my review of Jerry Mander's *Four Arguments for the Elimination of Television* in *The Structurist* in 1978 (see listing above)—epitomizes the opprobrium that has greeted numerous new media throughout history. "What is to be done with the motion picture shows . . . grinding out their reels of excitement and enchantment before the eyes of the motley throng of men and women, boys and girls?" McKeever cries out the Greek chorus of the ever-concerned, echoing the Socratic critique of writing (see the *Phaedrus*, listed below), contributing to the din that would later be echoed by Mander, Marie Wynn, Neil Postman (see listings above and below) and many others about television. "These moving pictures are more degrading than the dime novel," McKeever adds, "because they represent flesh-and-blood forms." The cellphone, because it conveys conversations between real people, who are in real settings such as cars and restaurants, has evoked new levels of attack, to the point of laws forbidding its use. Some, such as those forbidding cellphones in use in the hands of drivers, probably do make sense. Others, such as the one enacted by the New York City Council, over the Mayor's veto, fining use of cellphones in museums, are overkill—and, in view of the advent of texting, now unnecessary. This last point is the most important: shortcomings of media are best addressed not by new laws, but by new, remedial media that do better than the originals. See Chapter 11 in this book for technological remedies for some of the problems created by the cellphone.

McLuhan, M. (1962). *The Gutenberg Galaxy.* **New York: Mentor.**

The source of McLuhan's best-known, and probably best-understood, observation: "The new electronic interdependence recreates the world in the image of the global village" (p. 43). But both the global and the village part of the analogy were incomplete in 1962, and indeed through the 1960s and 1970s. Television was national, not international, and engendered a village of voyeurs, who could talk neither to one another nor to the town crier on the screen. The advent of cable television in the 1980s would make the village global, and the Web and cellphones in the 1990s would make it interactive. Meanwhile, the success of the "global village" and other McLuhan metaphors in the popular culture only angered many academics, allergic to original thinking, especially when not diced up with statistics. John Mackenzie, who met McLuhan at Fordham University in the late 1960s, relates a typical example in "The Slings and Arrows of Outrageous McLuhan," published in *Transactions of the Council on Medical Television* (1966): "An earlier draft of this paper was not simply rejected, it was repudiated. The editor of one journal . . . had a particularly inspiring and objective suggestion: 'If you have in mind to do another paper, on the fallacies of Professor McLuhan's assertions . . . then we would be happy to consider it for publication'." (Perhaps this is where McLuhan got the inspiration for his line in Woody Allen's 1973 *Annie Hall:* "You know nothing of my work—you mean my whole fallacy is wrong.") Mackenzie's paper is available at www.thewritingworks.com/mcluhan; see also my *Digital McLuhan,* listed above, for more on McLuhan's reception.

McLuhan, M. (1964). *Understanding Media.* **New York: Mentor.**

Still a treasure trove of brilliant, imaginative insights about numerous media, unique in its scope, depth, and capacity to provide what first seem like far-fetched but then on balance thoroughly plausible assessments of communication technologies and their impact. More than half of the times

I come up with an idea about media, I discover (and/or recall) that McLuhan was there first, in this book. Among the issues McLuhan raises about the telephone in his Chapter 27 ("The Telephone: Sounding Brass or Tinkling Symbol?"): "the telephone is an irresistible intruder in time or place"; "unlike radio, it [the telephone] cannot be used for background"; the call girl; the French phone; and the use of the word "phony" in a 1904 article in the *New York Evening Post* to mean insubstantial and untrustworthy, as in what you might hear on the phone. (See also my *Soft Edge*, p. 156—listed above—for the contribution of the Irish slang word "fawney" to the current "phony.") *Understanding Media* is also notable for its "medium is the message" observation (the way we communicate, the medium we use, is often overlooked in favor of the content, or what is communicated) and for the media analysis it gives such technologies as money, motor cars, and weapons; each of these and indeed every chapter in the book is packed with more ideas than are usually found in entire books devoted to the subject of the chapter.

McLuhan, M. (1976). "Inside on the Outside, Or the Spaced-Out American." *Journal of Communication* vol. 76, no. 4, pp. 46–53.

Presents, in a nutshell, the prime, intrinsic drawback of the cellphone: "Whereas we accept the phone as an invader of our homes. . . . The North American car is designed and used for privacy. . . . the motor car, then, for us is not only a means of transportation, but a way of achieving a deeply needed privacy. . . ." But that was in 1976, right before car phones and cellphones cracked the nut wide open, and left us no place to be private, not outdoors or indoors. So now, in 2003, there is no place under the sun, or incandescent or fluorescent light, where we can be unreachable. Our only recourse, as discussed here in Chapter 5, "The Drawbacks of Always Being in Touch," is to revise our social expectations about responsiveness to communication, to carve out times when we can be incommunicado without giving offense.

McLuhan, M. (1977). "Laws of the Media," with a preface by P. Levinson. *et cetera*, vol. 34, no. 2, pp. 173–79.

McLuhan here offers his "tetrad": Every technology, including media, has four kinds of impact:

1. It intensifies or amplifies, in the case of media, a particular mode of communication (e.g., radio intensifies instant one-way communication of sound across long distances).
2. It obsolesces or eclipses a mode of communication that had been amplified by an earlier medium (radio obsolesces the slower, indirect, visual delivery of news via printed newspapers).

3. It retrieves, or brings back into prominence, a mode of communication that previously had been eclipsed (radio retrieves the town crier as a deliverer of news, previously obsolesced by the newspaper).

4. Eventually, when pushed to its limits, a medium "flips" or reverses into a new medium, with characteristics quite opposite, or in contrast to, the original (sound-only radio flips into television with pictures).

This is just the bare bones of the tetrad. Reversal (the fourth effect) can retrieve elements that were previously obsolesced—so the reversal of radio into television retrieves some of the visual elements that radio eclipsed, and we're off and running with a new tetrad for television, which amplifies the immediate, long-distance, one-way audiovisual; obsolesces the immediate, long-distance, one-way, audio-only of radio; retrieves some of the visual obsolesced by radio; and reverses into holography (three-dimensional), videophone (two-way interactive), the Internet, movies-on-demand, et cetera. And we can, in turn, map out tetrads for each of these new media, with multiple elements amplified, obsolesced, and retrieved, and multiple reversals, as well. (Some of these aspects are explored in my "Tetradic Wheels of Evolution," a paper presented at the Tetrad Conference with Marshall McLuhan that I organized at Fairleigh Dickinson University in Teaneck, New Jersey, March 10, 1978; and see other papers presented at that conference; see also Marshall and Eric McLuhan, *Laws of Media* [Toronto: University of Toronto Press, 1988], for book-length treatment of the tetrad.) How about a tetrad for the cellphone: It amplifies instant, two-way communication from anywhere in the world to anywhere in the world; it obsolesces the tethers of wires that keep us and long-distance communication in rooms; it retrieves walking and talking in the outside world; and it reverses into texting, omni-accessibility limiting our freedom of communication as well as increasing it, and . . . well, having read this book and thought about the cellphone, you can probably fill in the blanks as well as I.

McNeill, W. H. (1982). *The Pursuit of Power*. Chicago: University of Chicago Press.

The author of *Plagues and Peoples* (New York: Doubleday, 1976), and its exploration of how micro-parasites have changed the outcomes of wars and the course of history, here looks at how "macro-parasites"—McNeill's apt term for humans preying on other humans—have shaped human civilization. In other words, this book is about war and all its concomitants. I cite the book because it provides a detailed description of the British Admiralty's initial mis-assessment of the value of steam power in naval operations in the 1820s—a telling example of the unreliability of experts in assessing and predicting the impact of new technology. (See Cherry's *Age of Access*, listed

above, for more.) McNeill also provides some details on the role of communications in military operations, observing that the telegraph "allowed an
advancing army to keep contact with distant headquarters simply by paying
out wire as it advanced," thereby strengthening the power of central command (p. 248). (Lincoln, we already have noted, directed Grant's every move
in the final stages of the war by telegraph.) A new chapter in McNeill's history needs to be added about the role of the cellphone in military campaigns.
(In the meantime, see Chapter 10 in the current volume for some preliminary
observations.)

McWilliams, P. A. (1982). *The Personal Computer Book.* Los Angeles:
Prelude Press.

An excellent, early snapshot of the personal computer, its capabilities, and
its impact. "It's a book for those who wonder what personal computers are,
what they have to offer, and what those offerings will cost. It's for people
who have had their 'computer literacy' questioned by such literary giants as
Time, Newsweek . . ." (p. 13). That included just about everyone in 1982. I
logged on to an online network for the first time in June 1984.

Meyrowitz, J. (1985). *No Sense of Place.* New York: Oxford University Press.

A classic on how television blurs distinctions between children and adults,
giving them access to the same information, and therefore leaving no one in
his or her right place. A cellphone in everyone's hand—child and adult—
greatly augments this process, by giving people access not only to the same
information, but, potentially, to the same people, since in cellphone-land
everyone is accessible by phone. But the packet of services provided by the
cellphone—not just conversations but, via its connection to the Internet,
eventually all that the Internet has to offer, ranging from movies to radio to
newspapers—means that the cellphone does not erase place, but rather
makes every place, anyplace, the place to be, as far as maximum choices in
communication. See Chapter 4 in the current volume, for more.

Mumford, L. (1934). *Technics and Civilization.* New York: Harcourt,
Brace, and World.

Although Mumford saw potential advantages and drawbacks in the new
media of his day—radio and motion pictures—he worried that "the dangers
of radio and the talking picture seem greater than the benefits" (p. 241).
Why? Because, as he explains a bit earlier (p. 240), the new speed and fuller
presence of long-distance communication has only "mobilized and hastened
mass reactions, like those which occur on the eve of war, and it has increased
the dangers of international conflict." Well, he was certainly prophetic about
Hitler and his use of radio and film. Mumford was not very happy about the
telephone, either, via which "the flow of interest and attention, instead of

being self-directed, is at the mercy of any strange person who seeks to divert it to his own purposes" (p. 240). For Mumford, then, separation—between public and private, between sending and receiving of information—was crucial to rational, civilized life. Although Mumford died in 1990, at ninety-four years of age, just prior to the real advent of the medium that most typified the immediacy that he so abjured—the cellphone—there is no doubt that, were he alive today, he would be its strongest (and most erudite and educated) critic. (Interestingly, Marshall McLuhan died an exact decade earlier—in 1980, at age sixty-nine—also on the very eve of the personal computer and Web revolutions that would bring into being the global village and fuller expressions of "acoustic space" that were at the center of most of *his* work. But where Mumford railed against the quickening of communication, McLuhan was neutral to positive about acoustic space. For Mumford's views of McLuhan, see immediately below.)

Mumford, L. (1970). *The Pentagon of Power.* **New York: Harcourt Brace Jovanovich.**

Mumford here reiterates his concerns about rampant immediacy—indeed, he quotes from the passage cited above written in 1934—and adds that the instantaneous, instantly effacing sounds and images of television are a "mass psychosis" (p. 294), with the same effect as "burning of the books" (because the content of television does not endure—even though video recording was more than a decade old at this time). Computers (in 1970, mainframe) come in for a lashing, too: they will encourage "total illiteracy, with no permanent record except that officially committed to a computer, and open to only those permitted access to this facility." Well, this was before personal computers in the home and hackers—though the former might well have also incurred Mumford's ire due to the immediacy of their operation and transmission. And mixed into all of this condemnation is a little diatribe on McLuhan—guilty of "trancelike vaticinations," and worse. "In the electronic phantasmagoria that he conjures up [this, presumably, is the global village?], not alone will old-fashioned machines be permanently outmoded [this is ipso facto bad?] but nature itself will be replaced [okay, that would be bad—but that's not at all happening; in fact, just the opposite, see my 'Human Replay,' listed above, and cellphones now get us out into the world]." Mumford concludes this part of his exposition of the destruction of healthy mental life by new media: "In McLuhan's case, the disease poses as the diagnosis." For McLuhan's part, he professed surprise at the vehemence of Mumford's attack. "What do you suppose he wants?" he once asked me, in the late 1970s, in his office in the Coach House at the University of Toronto. We discussed how McLuhan had always fairly and respectfully quoted and referenced Mumford, the older scholar, so that was not likely the problem. "I think basically he's just jealous of your success," I told McLuhan. I noticed, a little later during that visit, that Mumford's books did have a dubious place of honor in the Coach House, right up on one of the walls of its bathroom, on the second floor.

Münsterberg, H. (1916/1970). *The Photoplay: A Psychological Study.* **New York: Dover.**

Distracted from some of his usual work as a teacher of philosophy at Harvard University during World War I because of his German background, Münsterberg devoted his time to the study of film, and produced this marvelous work: an analysis of motion pictures in terms of Kantian philosophy; more specifically, how what we see on the screen, how we interpret various cinematic techniques such as close-ups, dissolves, and other ways of moving from one scene to another, are based on our innate Kantian modes of perceiving space, time, and causality (what Kant called "categories"). Münsterberg's result is both the first serious, philosophic assessment of film (in those days, the term "psychology" often was used interchangeably with "philosophy"—Münsterberg's Harvard colleague William James was both a philosopher and a psychologist) and an instructive application of Kant to our understanding of film and, by extension, twentieth-century communications. I say "instructive" because there are academics in many universities to this very day who deny or ignore the philosophic lessons in the structure and operation of media (including, no doubt, the cellphone).

Myers, J. (a.k.a. DeKnight, J.) and Freedman, M. (1952). "Rock Around the Clock."

First recorded in 1952 by Sonny Dae and His Knights, the song came to some prominence in 1954, when it was recorded by Bill Haley and the Comets. It was included in the soundtrack of the 1955 movie *Blackboard Jungle*, was re-released, and reached the top of the charts. Over the years, it has come to be considered the initiating anthem of rock 'n' roll. It certainly captured the kinetic power of the music, as well as its vividly sexual origins, and thus played perfectly out of radios in cars, which were also vehicles—literally—of the sexual revolution. As a boy in the 1950s, I loved the record but could never understand why Bill Haley or anyone would want to rock—dance—around the clock. I could see neither doing nor singing about it. When I later learned that the term "rock 'n' roll" was African American slang for sexual intercourse, I became a believer.

Peirce, C. S. (1896–1899). "The Scientific Attitude and Fallibilism," in J. Buchler, ed. *Philosophical Writings of Peirce.* **New York: Dover, 1955.**

Peirce, one of the most important yet under-recognized philosophers in history, here makes the crucial point that fallibilism, recognizing our inability to know everything, or anything with 100-percent precision, requires our being skeptical not only of what we think we know, but of what we're sure we do not and will not ever know. I term this "never-dogmatism," and it seems to crop up mostly in experts. There does not seem to be much harm done in the long run—Marconi invented the radio even though Hertz, the discoverer of electromagnetic waves, said it was not practically possible (see Cherry's *Age of Access*, listed above)—as long as outsiders, not in the know, are not prevented from pursuing their dreams.

Perrin, N. (1979). *Giving Up the Gun: Japan's Reversion to the Sword, 1543–1879.* **Boston: Godine.**

The refusal of Japanese samurai to use guns for over three hundred years is one of the few known cases in history of people declining to adopt a new technology (as opposed to being barred from using it by others). It's not as easy nowadays as then, though the Amish careful selection of technology is a significant example (see my "Amish Get Wired," listed above). So far, no culture—not the Japanese, not the Amish—have said no to the cellphone. To the contrary, everyone's snapping it up.

Phone Booth **(2003).**

This movie was directed by Joel Schumacher from the screenplay by Larry Cohen. One of the cellphone's clearest cultural casualties has been the public phone booth. Actually, the advent of the cellphone was a coup de grace for the phone booth, which had been stripped to its bare essentials since its heyday in the first half of the twentieth century, and was little more than a phone on a stalk in most places, anyway. *Phone Booth* purports to be about the last full-fledged glass-door phone booth in New York City, and sends the phone booth out in a cinematic blaze, if not of glory, of keen media savvy. Key ingredients in the plot are the irresistible ring of the phone, the conflict between talking on the phone and the people around you, and, most of all, the cellphone and its impact on marriage and infidelity. See Chapter 7 of the current book for more on that.

Plato (approx. 400 B.C.) *Phaedrus.*

Here, according to Plato's account, Socrates denounces the written word as disabling of our memories, an illegitimate image of the spoken original, and yearns for an "intelligent writing" that has the properties of speech, the capacity for immediate dialogue (in sections 275–76; see my "Intelligent Writing" and its listing above for a longer quote from the *Phaedrus*). Political leaders from Caesar (*Commentaries on the War in Gaul*) to Hitler (*Mein Kampf*) apparently agreed with the Socratic critique—yet all of them, including Plato, chose to write this down on inert paper. Indeed, if they had not, we would likely not know about their critiques of writing (well, we would probably know about Hitler's, because he talked a lot, in person and on radio, only seven decades ago), which is something of a self-defeating paradox in this position (using the very medium you condemn as unreliable, to make your point—something like the paradox of the liar, or "this statement is a lie"). In any case, text on computers and the cellphone would seem to satisfy most of Socrates' qualms, especially those regarding the unresponsive quality of words fixed to unrefreshable, unconnected (in today's parlance) objects like papyrus and walls, the only possible conveyors of writing back then. (The *Phaedrus* is an ancient tour de force of media theory in more ways than one. It also contains, at the beginning of section 275, Socrates' recounting of the Egyptian king Thamus of Thebes—already from bygone days—and Thamus' view that "he who has the gift of invention is not always the best judge of [its] utility or inutility." This is precisely the point made frequently in the current volume about the inaccuracy of Edison and others in predicting the use and impact of their inventions; see Cherry's *Age of Access*, listed above, for more. The invention that Thamus was alluding to, by the way, was writing, given to the Egyptians—invented—by an "old god," Theuth, according to Socrates in this account.)

Postman, N. (1992). *Technopoly: The Surrender of our Culture to Technology.* New York: Knopf.

Charmingly written—as are all of Postman's books—and much preferable to Jerry Mander's sledge-hammer and Marie Wynn's hyperbolic attacks on television (see listings above and below)—but an incorrect criticism of TV as destructive of literacy, nonetheless, with computers thrown in for blame in the bargain. Text on cellphones as well as computer screens refutes this claim. (Full disclosure: Postman was my doctoral advisor and mentor at New York University in the late 1970s. As his student, I tried in vain to correct his vision of electronic media. Perhaps because he earlier had a very different view about media and education—see his *Teaching as a Subversive Activity* [New York: Doubleday, 1969], which he wrote with Charles Weingartner—and had turned it around to be a media critic, he was chary to turn his views around again.) I dedicated this book to him, notwithstanding our different views of media, because he was the most gifted, dedicated, inspiring teacher I ever had.

Rheingold, H. (2003). *Smart Mobs: The Next Social Revolution.* Cambridge, MA: Perseus.

The social revolution considered here is primarily political. A good summary of the cellphone as a potent mobilizing instrument, especially in Asian and African nations and societies.

Rothman, W. (2003). "Gadget of the Week: Nokia 3650 Camera Phone." *Time* online edition, April 24. www.time.com/time/gadget/20030424

Schifferes, S. (2003). "Who Won the US Media War," *BBC News*, April 18. news.bbc.co.uk/go/pr/fr/-/2/hi/americas/2959833.stm.

Searle, J. R. (1980). "Minds, Brains, and Programs," in D. R. Hofstadter and D.C. Dennett, eds., *The Mind's I*. New York: Basic Books.

This essay distinguishes between "weak" and "strong" AI—artificial intelligence as auxiliary or augmenting of human intelligence vs. artificial intelligence as autonomous, thinking on its own behalf (as we do)—and argues against the possibility of ever creating the latter (autonomous artificial intelligence) short of creating a complete artificial being, "a machine with a nervous system, neurons with axons and dendrites, and all the rest of it, sufficiently like ours." I'm in complete agreement with the distinction—though I prefer the terms "auxiliary intelligence" and "autonomous intelligence" outright, over "weak" and "strong"—and in substantial agreement of the need of life as a prerequisite. As I noted in *Mind at Large*, listed above, to suggest that we can have autonomous artificial intelligence before artificial life is to put Descartes before the horse. On the other hand, also aware of the perils of "never dogmatism," I see no reason to shut the door completely on the possibility of disembodied intelligence, or intelligence outside of living systems. Such a development, after all, is not as intrinsically paradoxical as time travel. (See Chapter 3 in the current volume, and my "What Technology Can Teach Philosophy" in P. Levinson, ed., *In Pursuit of Truth: Essays on the Philosophy of Karl Popper* [Atlantic Highlands, NJ: Humanities Press, 1982] for more.)

Star Trek (1966–1969).

This was the original series, created by Gene Roddenberry, and broadcast on NBC-TV. Along with Dick Tracy's walkie-talkie wristwatch, the "communicator" on *Star Trek*, held in the hand, attached to the uniform, making a nice high-tech chirping sound, is the best-known predecessor of the cellphone in science fiction. Interestingly, we have made much more progress in communication since then than in transportation. We have barely even returned to the moon since 1969, and the Concorde supersonic transport has been retired by the British and the French. See my *Realspace*, 2003, listed above, for possible reasons for this dichotomy. Perhaps the cellphone, which gets us away from cyberspace perceived in rooms, to conversations and the Web while we walk and travel in the outside world, will help get us back on track in transportation, and eventually travel to the stars.

Swett, C. (2003). "The Ubiquitous Cellphone Turns 30." *Sacramento Bee*, April 12.

An excellent thumbnail social and technological history of the cellphone, with interviews and quotes from Martin Cooper (director of research and development for Motorola and responsible for its cellphone), Robert Thompson (professor of media and popular culture at Syracuse University), sundry users of the cellphone (a winery regional manager, a tennis pro, an advisor on business etiquette, a mortgage-loan processor, with varying opinions on the benefits, drawbacks, and future of the cellphone), and me. Just about all of the current book was written prior to this article, and I was interested to see that Thompson mentions some of the same impacts on family—and, of course, the role of the cellphone on September 11— discussed here.

Veblen, T. (1899/1953). *The Theory of the Leisure Class.* New York: MacMillan/Mentor.

This work contains Veblen's classic observation that being rich is not just its own reward—that being rich carries with it the heavy responsibility of demonstrating this wealth to the rest of the world, or, as Veblen terms it, "conspicuous consumption." In the early days of the cellphone, the nouveau riche—and the nouveau technological—no doubt enjoyed flaunting their phone conversations in public. This perhaps contributed to some of the irritation of onlookers—or "onlisteners" (maybe the cellphone has created a need for this new word)—though there were and are many other reasons (see Chapter 6 of the current book—"The Social Intruder"). In any case, cellphone subscriptions have now spread to over 50 percent of the population in the United States, making the cellphone unfit for any conspicuous consumption, except perhaps very briefly for kids when a phone with a cool new feature appears (such as phones that take videoclips).

Wachira, N. (2003). "Wireless in Kenya Takes a Village." *Wired News,* January 2. www.wired.com/news/wireless/0,1382,57010,00.html.

Wachowksi, L. & A. (1997/2001). *The Matrix—Shooting Script.* New York: Newmarket Press.

Wynn, M. (1977). *The Plug-In Drug.* New York: Viking.

Metaphors are useful, as long as we keep in mind their differences from reality—we're not likely, thinking that time flies, to find wristwatches right up there with birds in the sky. Is love really addicting? How many people other than Romeo and Juliet actually die from it? Is television in any real sense a drug, or is it a form of easy entertainment, with no palpable effect on our bodies? Whatever Wynn's conclusions about television—and I do not agree with them, for reasons given throughout the current book (see, for example, Chapter 8)—her title should be both commended for its flair but taken with a big grain of salt. (Is salt a drug? I don't think so—it's just a spice that's necessary to our diet.)

Young, J. (2003). "i h8 imspk (English: I hate Instant Messenger-speak)." *Behind the Curtains.* www.schoolofabraham.com/behindthecurtain.htm.

Zibart, E. (1999). "Rrring! rrring! rrring! Just when did the phone in your pocket become more irresistible than a real live person?" *Washington Post,* February 5.

Index

Printed in the United States
42205LVS00001B/177